A MOM JUST LIKE YOU

Vickie Farris
& Jayme Farris Metzgar

BROADMAN
& HOLMAN
PUBLISHERS

Nashville, Tennessee

A Mom Just Like You
Copyright © 2000, 2002 by Vickie Farris & Jayme Farris Metzgar

All rights reserved
Printed in the United States of America

Published by Broadman & Holman Publishers
Nashville, Tennessee

ISBN 0-8054-2586-1

Previously published by Loyal Publishing, Sisters, Oregon under same title as
ISBN 1-929125-10-0 (now OP)

Back cover photos Copyright © 2000 by Vickie & Jayme Farris
Cover design by Bill Chiaravalle

02 03 04 05 06 / 10 9 8 7 6 5 4

Contents

This book is dedicated to my husband, Mike,
who has loved me unconditionally and
has encouraged me tremendously
as a woman, wife, and mother.

Cast of Characters

Peter, born March 29, 1997. He has an exuberant personality, seems to be all energy, and prefers his own way. He never stops talking and eats up all the attention he gets as the youngest of ten.

Joseph, born September 27, 1993. Joey is our "Mr. Personality" and is almost always cheerful (sometimes to the point of being hyper!). He is very affectionate and is constantly singing.

Jonathan, born December 30, 1991. Johnny fluctuates between melancholy frustration and inspired delight. He is our "inventor," constantly exploring the way things work and the natural world.

Emily, born May 16, 1990. Stranded in the midst of the boys, Emily nevertheless holds her own. Although she is athletic and energetic, she is still flamboyantly feminine (much to her brothers' annoyance!).

Michael, born August 25, 1988. Michael is at the stage where he enjoys spending time with his friends and gravitates toward anything associated with computers. He has an affectionate and empathetic nature which peeks through the outer shell from time to time.

Angela, born February 3, 1987. Angie is famous for being the second mother of the household. Her steady, calm disposition (a rarity in this family!) has always drawn the youngest children to her for comfort. Angie has a sly, subtle sense of humor and is a talented athlete.

Jessica, born November 1, 1984. Like Angie (from whom she is inseparable), Jessica's imperturbable steadiness stands out in our family. She is a tremendous helper around the house, and she shares her love for books by reading aloud to the younger children. Jessica is talented artistically and musically, and she has recently become a part-time student at Patrick Henry College.

Katie, born August 31, 1980. An excellent athlete and a bit of a tomboy, Katie has always seemed more "grown-up" than her years. Just a few months after her high school graduation at age eighteen, she married Sean Dunn, a Texas native who came to Virginia as an intern for Home School Legal Defense Association (HSLDA), and who currently works for Patrick Henry College. Katie and Sean now live near us, along with their children Jenna Lee and Sean Charles Jr.

Jayme, born October 26, 1977. Jayme graduated early from high school and worked as a graphic designer at HSLDA until age nineteen. Her long-time interest in missions led her to Romania for the year in 1997, where she worked at both a Baptist college and a small orphanage. After returning home, she remained involved with the orphanage in Romania by founding a nonprofit organization to support its work with abandoned children. She also spent several months collaborating with me on this book in 1999. Jayme married Todd

Metzgar in June 2000, and they are expecting their first child in February 2002.

Christy, born June 28, 1975. Christy gained an interest in politics and journalism early, while working as the deputy press secretary for Mike's lieutenant governor campaign in 1993. The following year, she entered Cedarville College, where she maintained a 3.98 GPA, excelled in debate, became the Junior Class Vice President, and graduated *summa cum laude* with a degree in Political Science. In August 1998, Christy married her longtime best friend Rich Shipe, and they have since had three daughters: Emma Rose, Rachael Lynn, and Allie Kay. In addition to her mothering duties, Christy also finds time to write an advice column for your women on Crosswalk.com.

Mike, my husband. Mike lives in a whirlwind of activity. As founder, chairman, and general consel of Home School Legal Defense Association. Mike has dedicated years of his life to the home schooling movement, traveling the country to litigate cases and speak at home school conferences. More recently, his energies have been devoted to Patrick Henry College which opened its doors in September 2000 with Mike as its first president. Besides his "real job," Mike is also very active in state and national conservative politics, serves on the board of an international human rights organization, has published several books (most recently a series of Christian novels), serves as an elder in our church, and—lest we forget—is the father of ten. Despite all this activity, I am most proud of Mike for his walk with the Lord and his love for the Scriptures.

Jayme's Thoughts and Thanks

"I can't stand this chapter, I can't write this book, and I hate home schooling moms!" Those were my exact words, I'm sorry to say, after my fifth unsuccessful attempt at starting the first chapter of this book. While I immediately burst out laughing at the absurdity of my own statement, the discouragement I felt was still quite real.

Through prayer and the grace of God, however, chapter 1 was finally written, and Mom and I started seeing some progress. With each new chapter, it got a little easier to express the heart of another person. Despite the fact that I know Mom well, mentally "becoming" her both challenged me and gave me a whole new perspective—I truly felt that I was eventually able to share in her struggles, triumphs, and faith in God. By the time the book was nearing completion, I was thanking God for the honor of being given this chance to express my mother's heart.

Despite the frustrations, late nights, and loss of free time, I truly cannot think of anything more worthwhile to have done with my summer. For a long time, I have wanted the world to hear from Mom. To me, she is a unique person—both ordinary and extraordinary, down-to-earth and admirable. I believe this stems from the simple fact that she is a normal person, filled with the power and strength of an amazing God. As an aspiring home school mom myself, Mom's life encourages me that you don't have to be "super-mom" in order to raise a godly family. God can do extraordinary things with ordinary people!

Mom, for my part, I dedicate this book to you. The time I have spent working on it repays only the tiniest portion of what I owe you for pouring so much love, time, and energy into my life. It was truly a joy to work together with you, get a glimpse into your heart, and pray with you. (And, just for the record, I really do like home schooling moms—especially you.) I love you!

I also feel the need to thank the others who have contributed so much to the writing of this book. First, thanks to all of you who prayed, encouraged me, and understood when I had to work instead of spending time with you. Thanks to Dad and Bill Parker for the push and the vision—especially to Dad for lending me the laptop! Thank you, Loyal Publishing, for believing in this book before we did, and for that one-month extension.

Many thanks to all the people who let me borrow their computers (you know who you are), especially Suzanne and Christy. Thank you, Jessica and Angie, for doing all that babysitting! Thanks to Christy, Katie, Ruth, and Jane for being my "mental audience."

Thank you, Todd, for bearing the brunt of my fatigue and discouragement, and for rejoicing with me when I rejoiced. Thanks for listening, praying with me, and bringing me dinner once in a while, but mostly for pointing me back to the true Author and Finisher of my faith.

Thank You, Lord Jesus, for being my Life and Light, and for answering those tearful late-night prayers. And thank You for a mother who loves You and serves You with her whole being.

Jayme Farris Metzgar

Now to Him who is able to do exceeding abundantly beyond all that we ask or think, according to the power that works within us, to Him be the glory in the church and in Christ Jesus to all generations forever and ever. Amen.

EPHESIANS 3:20-21

Introduction

ORDINARY MOMS DON'T HAVE TIME TO WRITE BOOKS

Actually, My Daughter Wrote This One

Vickie, I just had another call asking if you would speak at a home school conference with me. What do you think?"

Mike had already tried several times to get me to speak at home school conferences, but I had been too overwhelmed with my responsibilities at home to even consider the idea. I was so busy teaching, nursing babies, running after toddlers, and trying in vain to keep up with the laundry, that the idea of preparing a coherent speech in the midst of it all seemed absolutely out of the question!

"Besides, Mike," I protested, "who am I to try to tell these women how to do all this? I haven't figured that out myself yet!" I felt absolutely unqualified as a speaker. All the women I had ever heard speak at conferences seemed to know all the answers and run their households at least as smoothly as the Proverbs 31 woman— maybe even better! I knew I was no expert, and I certainly did not have all the answers on how to be the perfect wife and mother.

"But, Vickie," Mike argued, "that's just it! It would encourage these moms to hear from someone like you, who struggles and gets discouraged just like they do. And yet you've stuck with it for sixteen years now, and you know that you've experienced some tremendous rewards from it all. These women need to hear your story!"

Well, Mike certainly did not become a lawyer for nothing—he is a very effective advocate! He did manage to talk me into several speaking engagements, but with my houseful of children to care for, my speaking opportunities had to remain very limited.

As Mike continued to travel throughout the country speaking to home school audiences, however, he heard an oft-repeated comment from the women: "We enjoyed your message tremendously, and we were very encouraged, but we would really like to talk to your wife! How does she do it all?"

Mike came home from one of these conferences with an idea. "Vickie, I think you should write a book! These moms really want to hear from you."

I just laughed, feeling very much like Sarah when she heard the Lord tell Abraham that she would be blessed with a child in her nineties. "Mike, you're crazy! There is no way I have time to write a book. I can't even keep up with my thank-you notes!"

My Idea Man was not to be discouraged, however. "I've got it, Vickie! We'll have Jayme write the book, and we'll call it Ordinary Home School Moms Don't Have Time to Write Books, with the subtitle 'Actually, My Daughter Wrote This One.'"

"Hm-m-m. That's a weird title, but it certainly is true. And not only do I not have time to write a book, I don't even have time to think about it, even if Jayme did agree to write it—and I don't think she will." I could be persistent, too, and I persisted in dismissing the idea whenever it came up.

Realizing that he was not making much headway with me, Mike turned to others for some help. He shared his idea with our good friend Bill Parker, a home schooling father of eleven and the CEO of Crosswalk.com, a Christian website. Bill, who is a visionary like Mike, liked the idea immediately. Now Mike had a partner in persuasion!

Because Bill is an elder in our church, Jayme and I inevitably ran into him every Sunday. And Bill certainly is Mike's match when it comes to persuasion. Despite our efforts to avoid him, Bill would always seek us out. "Hey, Vickie! Have you started that book yet? You really need to write it—it's a great idea. People need this book!! Now Jayme, I want to see an outline from you by next Sunday, okay?" Although we were somewhat skeptical in the face of Bill's enthusiasm, Jayme and I did make some effort to comply with his request. However, we had a hard time getting started and soon gave up in discouragement.

Finally, Mike took his idea and our outline to his friend and publisher, Matt Jacobson. Much to my astonishment, he liked the idea too! Jayme and I were beginning to wonder if maybe God really did want us to write this book. As we prayed and struggled with the idea, we began to think that maybe—just maybe—we could pull it off.

Jayme would have to give up some of her other activities for a while and focus on writing the book. But with summer almost upon us, our teaching responsibilities would be temporarily completed (Jayme was helping me teach our two youngest school-age boys). We decided that we could potentially find the time to do the writing.

We soon found ourselves signing a contract. "Just what are we getting into?" I thought, as I signed my name on the documents. "Can we really do this?" I wondered. The one thought that comforted me was the fact that Jayme had previously helped me with some writing responsibilities, and I knew her to be an excellent writer who was able to capture on paper precisely my thoughts and feelings.

I can't deny that Jayme and I had our difficulties in writing this book. We had a very hard time getting started, and as I read over some of Jayme's early efforts, I felt a knot developing in my stomach. "Oh no, this just isn't what I want to say. But I don't know how to organize or express what really is on my heart!"

"Help!" I cried to Mike. "I just don't know how we should start this book, and I don't know what to tell Jayme!" Mike sat down with the two of us and helped us tremendously with the task of clarifying and organizing our thinking. He also suggested some important points that he thought we ought to include in our first two chapters.

I realized I needed to give Jayme much more input than I had originally done. Jayme and I decided we would need to discuss beforehand each chapter in detail, with me supplying illustrations, Scriptures, and important ideas for her to expand upon. And then the two of us went to the Lord in prayer, asking Him to guide our thinking and writing, to help us work together well, and to use this book to bless and encourage the women who would read it. I remember that I was cleaning out the garage, and I asked Jayme to come out and talk to me as I cleaned. Then the two of us sat on the garage steps to pray together, even as a thunderstorm hit and I watched the rain pour down on all the things I had moved out onto the driveway!

After our rough beginnings, things went much more smoothly—the Lord indeed is good! Even though we were inevitably interrupted by fighting little boys and various crises that always seemed to occur just as we were sitting down to go over a chapter together, we felt that we were able to make consistent progress, and the ideas and illustrations seemed to come easily.

Jayme is truly the author of most of this book. We both agreed, however, that I needed to write chapters 3 and 4, which deal with birth control, miscarriage, and menopause. Those two chapters, along with this introduction, are the only portions of the book written completely by me. Just taking on the entirety of those chapters proved to be a challenge for me, since quiet moments are extremely rare. I finally decided I had to get out of the house, and I spent several days in the solitude of the public library, writing the chapters in a notebook. Sometimes I even went outside and sat in our van to get away from the noise and concentrate on my writing!

I also extensively edited and actually wrote several portions of the chapter on husbands. In regard to this particular chapter, Jayme's quite accurate comment was, "It's very hard to write about something that I have no practical experience with whatsoever!" Most of what Jayme did write in that chapter came from the outline of a speech I gave on "The Top Two Priorities of Home School Moms," as well as an article I wrote for a home school magazine. The speech on priorities supplied much of what she wrote in chapter 7, also. Another speech outline supplied information for chapters 5 and 6.

Despite the fact, however, that I supplied Jayme with these outlines, some of my other writings, and the key concepts for each chapter, there were many times when I simply gave her a jumble of unorganized notes and thoughts to work with. I would try to find quiet moments to organize and write down my ideas for her, but I did not always succeed. With our busy household, along with the fact that this summer also included the births of two granddaughters and an addition to our house, I often gave up in frustration and sent Jayme off with a minimum of input. I was then totally amazed when Jayme would come back to me with a wonderfully written chapter that expressed exactly what I wanted to say, in a way that was even better that I could have said it! Jayme has had an incredible ability to take my ideas, express them in a way that I would want to express them, and then add some thoughts of her own that served to clarify and enhance my original ideas.

Moreover, whenever I did need to tell Jayme that what she had written was not quite what I wanted to say or was not the way I wanted to say it, she seemed to immediately understand my corrective comments. She was always able to revise her writing to conform perfectly to my thoughts.

Because, and only because, the Lord provided Jayme and her talents at just the right time, I have been able to take care of my busy family and "write" a book that truly expresses my heart. I want to thank Jayme for her willingness to give up her summer and most of her free time to help me with this book. It has been a true joy to work with Jayme; she has been tremendously gracious, patient, and diligent in her work, even when she struggled at times with weariness and discouragement. Thank you so much, Jayme—I love you!

I also want to thank Mike and Bill for "nagging" Jayme and me to write this book. If for no other reason, this book has already blessed Jayme and me tremendously as we have reviewed what God has done in and through our family. If you want to be truly encouraged, take some time to reflect back on the many things God has given you, done for you, and been to you. I am sure you'll be both surprised and uplifted, as we have been.

I am also excited to have a written record of what God has done to pass on to my children, grandchildren, and generations to come. Imagine how wonderful it would be to read something written by your great-great-grandmother, telling how God had worked in her life and the things He had taught her. What a precious spiritual inheritance that would be!

My deepest desire for this book, however, is to encourage you in your role as a mother. I looked up the word "encourage" in the dictionary, and the precise meaning is "to inspire with courage, spirit, or confidence; to stimulate by assistance; to hearten, reassure, support, help." My prayer is that this book will do all of those things for you!

Contrary to popular belief, being a stay-at-home mom is not an easy thing to do. And when you add home schooling to the equation, it becomes even harder. There is much opportunity for discouragement, weariness, doubts about your own competency as a mother and teacher, loneliness, and perhaps even feelings of worthlessness. "Here I am, stuck in my house, changing diapers and trying to teach little ones—what am I doing to really make a difference?" we might think. "How am I helping others or reaching the world for Christ? I'm not even doing a good job where I am! My kids are always fighting, they seem to have trouble with the easiest lessons, my house is always a mess, and I seem to be accomplishing very little. Maybe I'm just not cut out for this."

Adding insult to injury, we may see or hear about other women who seem to be able to "do it all"—home school their children using the classical education method, run their homes with precision, sew all their children's clothing, and then travel the country speaking about it at conferences. Looking at these women, we think, "What is wrong with me, anyway? There is no way I could do all that!"

I'll tell you something: I have thought that very thing many times. I think there really are some talented, energetic women out there, whom God has gifted in a special way and who really can do all those things—but I'm not one of them. I am a very normal mom who happens to have a very visible, talented, and energetic husband. Okay, we do have a larger-than-normal family, too, but I am still learning how to manage it!

I struggle regularly with feeling overwhelmed, and I have days when I want to quit. I constantly ask the Lord to help me get on a better, more disciplined schedule, and I struggle to be consistent with my quiet time. I am not the super-mom you might have imagined me to be—the very nature of this book is proof of that. A super-mom could certainly write her own book! I am very much a mom just like you. And from one normal mom to another, let me just tell you that God is faithful, and if you "commit your way to the LORD" and "trust also in Him," then "*He* will do it!" (Psalm 37:5, emphasis added). That is exactly what He has done for me. I have determined to trust Him when the going gets tough, I have cried out to Him for help and wisdom, and I have clung to His Word through it all—and He has given the success.

Yes, it is hard; yes, sometimes it's lonely; yes, there is much weariness; yes, sometimes you feel like you just can't go on. But Scripture reminds us that "the LORD is my shepherd; I shall not want. *He* maketh me to lie down in green pastures; *he* leadeth me beside the still waters. *He* restoreth my soul: *he* leadeth me in the paths of righteousness for *his* name's sake" (Psalm 23:1-3, KJV, emphasis added). And the rewards He gives are worth it all in the end! Just one example from my own life is a daughter who loves the Lord, who writes well, who is one of my best friends, and who knows me well enough to express my very heart in this book. I believe she will be one of ten such precious gifts when my work is done!

You have much to look forward to, if you simply remain faithful to what God has called you to do. I hope my story gives you the courage and confidence to keep going. I pray that some of the lessons the Lord has taught me along the way will give you a measure of support and help for the tasks that you face. Most of all, I pray that you will keep your eyes on the One who "will continually guide you, and satisfy your desire in scorched places, and give strength to your bones," so that "you will be like a watered garden, and like a spring of water whose waters do not fail" (Isaiah 58:11). Yes, you have much to look forward to if you remain faithful. I know, because that has been my experience, and I'm a mom just like you.

But God has chosen the foolish things of the world to shame the wise, and God has chosen the weak things of the world to shame the things which are strong.

1 Corinthians 1:27

1

DISPELLING THE MYTH OF SUPER MOM

How God Chose an Unlikely Candidate for This Job

The grocery checkout line didn't seem to be moving. I looked impatiently at my watch, thinking of my children who were waiting (and probably fighting) in the van. It had been a long day, and as I finally approached the checker, it was difficult to return her friendly smile. My two-year-old son Peter, however, greeted her with a cheerful "hi!"

Smiling at Peter, the checker turned to me. "How old is he?" she asked. "Is he your first child?"

"No," I said, smiling in spite of myself. "Actually, to tell you the truth, he's my tenth."

"Your tenth!" She looked at me more closely, shaking her head in amazement. "I don't know how you do it. I only have two children, and they drive me crazy! You must be the most patient, organized woman in the world."

I laughed to myself, reviewing the day's events in my mind. First, I had wakened later than I had planned, because I had stayed up too late the previous evening. Walking downstairs and into the kitchen, I had discovered that Peter had emptied half of the Cheerios box on the kitchen floor, and that Joey had a slight fever. The day had continued in a similar fashion, with multiple quarrels between children, a frantic search for the van keys, and a scraped knee in the Wal-Mart parking lot. Now, standing impatiently in a grocery line listening to the sound of my head throbbing, I was faced by a woman calling me "the most patient, organized woman in the world."

"No, not really," I smiled. "It's not that I'm all that patient or organized. It's pretty much just the grace of God that gets me through." It was a simple answer, but a complete one.

It is common for outsiders to assume that a home schooling mother of a large family must be naturally qualified for the job. Contrary to this assumption, however, I have never had any asset except the grace of God. I started my married life with no natural abilities as a housekeeper, seamstress, cook, or even as a mother. In fact, as I look back, I believe I was probably the least likely candidate for this job.

I grew up an only child. My mother ran her house with innate German orderliness, providing our family with excellent meals and immaculate surroundings. I was somewhat spoiled and a little bit lazy, enjoying the outdoors and play much more than housework and helping my mom. I never had the desire to learn cooking or sewing, and I left for college without knowing how to prepare a meal. When I married, however, I quickly saw the benefit of such knowledge. I remember calling my mom in desperation, asking, "What do I do with the raw meat?" Even, today, cooking is not my favorite activity, and I never did pick up sewing.

In addition to my lack of domesticity, my childhood provided me with very little experience handling babies or young children. I clearly remember visiting my cousin Nancy shortly after the birth of her first son. I was in my early teens, and I looked at my new little second cousin with a mixture of fear and bewilderment. I nearly panicked when he was placed into my arms (it didn't help that he began to scream almost immediately). "What do I do with this baby?" I remember thinking. "I'm afraid I'll break him!" It was Mike who first taught me how to fold and change a diaper after the birth of our first child!

My organizational skills have never been particularly exceptional. Although necessity has taught me to become fairly organized, our house is still often a place of frantic searches for keys, warranties, Lego men, and soccer shoes—all very recent examples. I have been known to write letters and leave them lying untouched on my desk for months. I have yet to master the skill of training my children to pick up after themselves without continual prodding from me.

Neither do I see myself as being innately qualified for the job of lawyer-politician's wife. I have always been naturally shy, and it is somewhat of a stretching experience to attend political functions and dinners with my husband. I never had a natural interest in law of politics—my least favorite subject in school was government.

I also tend to be somewhat of a scaredy-cat when Mike is traveling overnight, policing the house to make sure that all the doors and windows are securely locked. I have even been known to look inside the clothes dryer for hiding intruders, much to the amusement of my husband and children!

So just how did I go from being a shy, nondomestic only child to being the mother of ten children and wife of a nationally-known home school leader? The story starts and ends with God, and God alone. He changed my direction, rechanneled my desires, and brought success instead of defeat. The words of the apostle Paul in 1 Corinthians 1:26-31 seem to describe my life perfectly:

> For consider your calling, brethren, that there were not many wise according to the flesh, not many mighty, not many noble; but God has chosen the foolish things of the world to shame the wise, and God has chosen the weak things of the world to shame the things which are strong, and the base things of the world and the despised, God has chosen, the things that are not, that He might nullify the things that are, that no man

should boast before God. But by His doing you are in Christ Jesus, who became to us wisdom from God, and righteousness and sanctification, and redemption, that just as it is written, "LET HIM WHO BOASTS, BOAST IN THE LORD."

Today, I find myself in a unique position to fully experience the truth of this passage. With so many young children still at home, I am daily reminded of my own weakness and foolishness apart from God. Like other home schooling mothers, I doubt my capability as a mother and a teacher, and I worry over the weaknesses I see in the lives of my children. I am fully able to identify with "the lowly things of this world and the despised things."

However, with three grown daughters and two more rapidly approaching adulthood, I am been able to clearly see the other side of the equation: that God's power can "nullify the things that are" and produce extraordinary results. I can look back and remember the weaknesses and failings of my three oldest daughters, and see firsthand how God was able to transform them in answer to my prayers.

OUR SMALL "SUCCESS STORIES"

For many years I worried about my oldest daughter, Christy, and her lack of diligence. Although she was capable, bright, and popular, she was often lazy when it came to her schoolwork and chores. She was famous for "mysterious disappearances" whenever it came time to clean up after dinner. In spelling, her weakest subject, she seemed unmotivated to study and improve.

As Mike and I worked to emphasize diligence and teach good study habits, we saw some gradual progress. But when Christy left for college at the age of nineteen, I was somewhat worried. I felt that, in a sense, our home school experiment was finally being put to the test. Christy had not been in a traditional school since first grade. Would she know how to study, and would she apply herself to the task? Would she do well in a classroom setting? Would the fact that we had not taught much science prove to be a handicap? Would she do well socially?

I need not have worried. From the very beginning, Christy's college career was marked by hard work and success. There were times she even surprised me by excelling in areas that had traditionally been weak for her. I remember getting a phone call from Christy one day in her junior or senior year. "Mom, guess what?" she said. "I got the only perfect score on our impossible Earth and Space Science test! About half the class failed, but I managed to get a 100!"

"Wow, Christy, I'm...amazed!" I replied. "I mean, we never really taught you a whole lot of science."

"I know," she said. "But I just studied."

Christy joined the debate team and soon began distinguishing herself as an excellent debater. Although we well knew that Christy was skilled in speaking (and speaking forcefully!), her diligence in researching each debate topic was particularly rewarding to see. Her grades also reflected good study skills—she achieved an overall grade point average of 3.98, earning the Outstanding Graduate Award from the National Educational Debate Association.

Mike and I were also gratified to see that Christy had a very healthy social life at college. She made many good friends and served as student body vice president in her junior year. In June 1998, Christy graduated *summa cum laude* with a degree in Political Science, and a minor in English. While it was highly rewarding to witness her achievements at college, it was even more rewarding to see the character development in her life that had made those achievements possible. She had gone from being a somewhat lazy, irresponsible child to an adult who took initiative and sought excellence.

Today, Christy continues to keep herself busy. As a wife and new mother, she runs the Home School Legal Defense Association's debate program from her home. She and her husband, Rich Shipe, have also taken on the responsibility of leading the church youth group, along with another newlywed couple. As I look at Christy's life, I can clearly see God's hand, as well as His answers to prayer. I know my own weaknesses too well to give myself credit for her success. I can only thank God that He took the seeds Mike and I planted, nourished them, and caused them to grow and produce fruit.

My second daughter, Jayme, had almost the opposite problem that Christy had. While Christy was friendly and easy-going to the point of laziness, Jayme was conscientious and insecure to the point of perfectionism. No grade but an A+ was high enough, and almost no praise was profuse enough to keep her from crying over her "failure." I remember several years when Jayme's whiny insecurity required a great deal of patience on my part. While she was an excellent, creative student, and I never worried about her academic abilities, I wondered whether such an emotionally fragile child could ever make it socially. I feared that Jayme, overshadowed by Christy's bright personality, would never come into her own.

Once again, my fears were proved unfounded by achievement far beyond my expectations. Jayme gradually became more relaxed and stable in her teen years, distinguishing herself in ballet and graduating from high school at the age of fifteen. However, she truly began to blossom after Christy left for college in 1994. Jayme had begun working as a graphic designer at Home School Legal Defense Association, and she quickly began to show great promise in that field. What's more, she began developing many friendships and showing surprising leadership among her peers.

In 1995 Jayme experienced what she calls a "spiritual growth spurt," where she began making God a part of her daily life and truly hungering after the Scriptures. She renewed a childhood interest in missions, and in 1996 she traveled to Romania for a five-week missions trip. She fell in love with the Romanian people, and in January 1997, at the age of nineteen, she moved to Romania as a missionary for one year. While there, she served as the International Relations Secretary for Dr. Paul Negrut, president of Emmanuel Bible Institute of Oradea, which required her to coordinate the college's relations with the English-speaking world. On weekends she volunteered at Hope House Family Center, a small, private home for abandoned babies.

At the end of 1997, despite the fact that Jayme had been asked to stay an additional year in Romania, she decided that God wanted her to return home to help me. Since that time, she has been living at home and has taken on the responsibility of home schooling Jonathan and Joseph. She also started her own nonprofit organization, Regeneration Ministries, to support the small orphanage at which she worked in Romania. Jayme has been very active in our church, serving as Sunday school teacher, Awana leader, missions committee member, drama team member, and choir member. Most recently, she has been working with me as ghostwriter for this book.

Jayme's social life, about which I once worried, now worries me for the reason that it is almost too full! At age twenty-two she has already been a bridesmaid in five weddings, and she is busy almost every day with phone calls, lunch appointments, and e-mail correspondence with friends on both sides of the Atlantic. She also surprises me with her public speaking ability, where she was once so insecure and withdrawn. I believe Jayme, like Christy, was transformed due to her relationship with God. Once she felt secure in His unchanging love, she was able to put aside self-consciousness and focus on the needs of others.

Katie, my third daughter, was probably my most difficult child in her early years. She had a very strong will and would often clash with me over schoolwork assignments. Her personality was an unusual mix. She had some of Christy's stubborn independence, some of Jayme's sensitivity, and an athletic tomboyishness that was purely her own. Katie's personality often clashed with Mike's, and for a while we were rather worried about how she would turn out. Even today, she agrees with us that she was the most likely candidate to become the family "black sheep." We feared she would reject our values and run off with a wild young man to join a motorcycle gang!

However, in Katie's high school years, things gradually began to change. Because she had always been a talented athlete, Mike and I decided to enroll her in the sports program at our local Christian school, which welcomes home schoolers. For four years she participated in softball, basketball, and track, alongside the Christian school students.

At first, Mike and I worried about the influence of some of Katie's Christian school friends. While some of them were near Katie's level of maturity, others came from troubled homes and had been sent to the school as a way of reforming them. At one point, we seriously considered removing Katie from her involvement in sports because of the potential for negative influence. But then a remarkable thing began to happen: we saw Katie emerging as a leader among her friends at the Christian school. Rather than being influenced, she began to influence them. In fact, we later discovered that it was not until Katie saw the troubled lives of some of her friends that she actually began to adopt our values as her own. Everything Mom and Dad had been telling her all along suddenly began to make sense. By the time she reached her senior year of high school, her beliefs were so solidified that we were able to confidently send her to the local community college for several courses.

It was also in Katie's high school years that she began a very positive, godly friendship with Sean Dunn, an

HSLDA intern. As young as she was, Katie had always seemed older than her years in many ways. Sean, who was three years her senior, soon became her closest friend (much to Mike's delight). Far from being the motorcycle-riding delinquent we had always feared for Katie, Sean was somewhat quiet, fun loving, home schooled, and a very polite and respectful young man. When he asked to court Katie in 1997, Mike enthusiastically agreed.

Katie and Sean were married in October 1998, and they had their first daughter (our second granddaughter), Jenna Lee Dunn, on August 30, 1999. Every day I have been impressed by Katie's patient handling of her pregnancy and new motherhood, and by the delight she seems to take in her domestic responsibilities. Although she is still a tomboy at heart (she and Sean coached softball this spring, pregnancy and all), Katie has also taken up cooking, home decorating, and even cross-stitching with talent and flair. More importantly, she has become a loving and submissive wife and a patient and caring mom. We praise God for His evident hand in her life.

I believe that my next two daughters, like their three older sisters, are well on their way to living lives of service for God. Jessica, who is now fifteen, and Angela, thirteen, are currently my most faithful helpers at home. They are responsible with the younger children and relatively uncomplaining when it comes to household chores. Although I do not want to give the impression that they are perfect, they do show a very encouraging maturity and a willingness to serve.

Despite my own weakness, then, my older children serve as daily reminders of God's strength. When I look at my little ones, with their selfish tendencies, petty quarrels, and laziness, I am heartened to remember that Christy, Jayme, and Katie had similar weaknesses at the same age.

WHAT TO EXPECT FROM THIS BOOK

I have already emphasized that it was God, not I, who brought about spiritual success in the lives of my children. I have no twelve-step, one-size-fits-all formula for producing great kids, nor do I believe that such a formula exists. While I will share with you some of the practical aspects of how we handled our schooling, housework, and childrearing, I want you to know that I am not proposing that every family do exactly what we did. Individual families require individual methods. The last thing I want is for home schooling moms to pattern their schedules, curriculum, and methods after mine. That is certainly not the purpose of this book.

My main reason for writing this book is to share with you several specific, basic spiritual lessons I have learned over the past seventeen years of home schooling. These were the truths that kept me going on the days when I felt like quitting, and which enabled me to model the trust in God that I wanted to see in my children. I believe they are applicable to almost anyone because, rather than being human formulas for success, they are simply ways to stay focused on God and "tap into" His divine strength. As I tell the story of my home schooling and mothering experience, these are the themes you will see emerging again and again.

First, I have learned to take God at His word. James tells us that "faith without works is dead" (James 2:26).

As a mother, I have learned to have a living faith by claiming the truth of God and acting as if it were a certainty. God has promised that when I wait for Him, I will renew my strength (Isaiah 40:31). Do I act accordingly? He has told me that children are a blessing and a reward from Him (Psalm 127:3). Do I really believe that? God has said that I will reap a harvest in due time, if I do not give up (Galatians 6:9). Do I expectantly await the fulfillment of that promise? Taking God at His word is a lesson that spills over into all areas of life, including motherhood and home schooling. Throughout this book, I will tell you specific truths that have been meaningful to me and how God has been faithful to fulfill them.

Second, I have maintained the vision of raising a godly seed and remember the importance of motherhood. Many of us stay-at-home moms are often tempted to feel that our lives are useless or unimportant. Because today's women are valued most for their achievements outside the home, that feeling increases. I felt this way especially during my early days of motherhood, when my children were small and I was doing little but changing diapers, feeding babies, and caring for toddlers all day long. I used to worry that my children were hindering me from doing the really important work that God wanted me to do. It has been the vision of raising godly seed that had kept me from discouragement. As thrilled as I am to see my children serving Christ, it excites me even more to think of my grandchildren and great-grandchildren continuing that service to Him. Imagine the impact on our nation if every American Christian family could simply pass on its faith to each successive generation! It is this vision—the vision of a righteous family growing into a righteous nation—that has kept me going on some of the most monotonous, tiring days. I pray that this book will help you to catch that same vision.

Third, I have learned to pray for my children. No mother is perfect, nor can she possibly foresee the precise plan God has for her children. As I work to teach my children both academically and spiritually, I sometimes worry about my ability to fully equip them for their future lives. Should I focus more on science or history or public speaking or foreign languages? How can I know what skills they will need in the future? I have continually made it a habit to pray that God would cover over my mistakes and equip each child as He sees fit. He knows exactly what each of my children will do in the future, and He is able to ensure that each child is fully prepared for the task. I have also consistently prayed that God would lead each of my children to a godly spouse in His timing. But without a doubt, my most fervent prayer for each child has simply been that he or she would have a close walk with God. The desire of my heart is that my children will be closer to God, and more fully His, than Mike and I have been.

God has graciously answered my prayers thus far. I have seen Him prepare Christy, Jayme, and Katie for the current work in areas I could never have foreseen. I have seen Him lead Christy and Katie into marriage with godly husbands, and Jayme into courtship with a godly young man. Finally, I have seen each of my oldest daughters walking with God far more deeply than I did at their ages. I am sure that the spiritual success of my daughters stems from answered prayers more than any other cause. As I share my story with you, you will hear more of God's miraculous answers to prayer.

Fourth, I have learned to put my relationship with God first. Although this is still a daily struggle, and I have yet to fully put into practice what I know, I firmly believe that I have made it this far simply because I have spent time with God. How can I be a successful mom if I am walking in my own flesh and not in the Holy Spirit? And how can I expect my children to put God first if I don't model what I'm teaching?

"They that wait upon the LORD shall renew their strength," Isaiah tells us. "They shall mount up with wings as eagles; they shall run and not be weary; and they shall walk, and not faint" (Isaiah 40:31, KJV). Without a doubt, home schooling a large family requires strength. Don't believe anyone who would try to tell you it's an easy job. However, I have seen that when I wait upon the Lord, my work is both *possible* and *worthwhile*. It requires the Lord's strength, to be sure. But any work done in the Lord's supernatural strength will yield His supernatural results. I pray you will be encouraged as I share with you the abundant harvest He has thus far given me.

For it is God who is at work in you, both to will and to work for His good pleasure.

PHILIPPIANS 2:13

2

WHY AM I DOING THIS ANYWAY?

The Importance of a Solid Foundation

I threw aside my teacher's manual and marched out of the room. "Forget it, girls, just forget it!" I yelled, hurrying upstairs toward my bedroom before the tears of frustration spilled over. At the top of the staircase I stopped and looked down at my daughters, who had sheepishly followed me out into the hallway. They stood gaping at me, their recent quarrel completely forgotten.

"We're not home schooling anymore," I said with finality. "I'm sending you all to public school!" Slam went my bedroom door, and then all was quiet. I finally broke down and let the angry tears come.

Just two weeks earlier, I had started the school year bursting with enthusiasm. I was full of new, creative ideas and anxious to try them out. But as we began home schooling that year, I found that my daughters did not share my enthusiasm. Their griping and complaining about the new materials was exceeded only by their fighting with one another. Suddenly, the coming school year lost all its promise, looming ahead like a gray, dreary, never-ending mist. I just did not think I could face it. How bad could it be to send our children to public school?

My daughters were distraught over this idea. As my own tears subsided, I could hear the three of them downstairs—Katie sniffling, Jayme sobbing, and Christy loudly protesting that it couldn't happen, they'd see. Although I was somewhat moved by their reluctance to go to public school, I still didn't think I had the heart to make it through the rest of the year. Could home schooling possibly be worth all this trouble and headache?

Mike came home that night to a disturbed household. Almost the instant he walked in the door, the children greeted him with the day's big news: "Guess what, Dad? Mom said she's not going to home school us anymore, and we all have to go to school!" As Mike glanced at me, my grim face and reddened eyes served as confirmation of this report. "You and I need to go somewhere and talk...privately," his look said. I took the hint, and just after dinner we retreated upstairs for a closed-door conference.

I was the first to talk, spilling out all my pent-up complaints. "I just don't think I have the energy for this anymore!" I told him. "I mean, it would be one thing if I could see some results, some indication that all this work is actually worth it. But all I ever see is complaining and fighting! Why am I doing this anyway?"

I finally ran out of steam. Mike looked at me for a minute and finally said, "That's a good question, Vickie. Why are we doing this? Do you remember the reason we started home schooling in the first place?" I returned his gaze steadily, thinking back to the very beginning, when we first started home schooling.

It really began in 1980. Our family was living in Spokane, Washington, at the time, where Christy (5), Jayme (3), and Katie (1 month) had been born. Although Mike and I were planning to move to Olympia, Washington, I prepared to send Christy to the local public kindergarten during our last two months in Spokane. Since the school was just a few blocks away from our house, we would walk there together each morning. The half-day of school went by quickly, and Christy would come home to play for the rest of the afternoon.

When our family moved from Spokane to Olympia in November 1980, Mike and I found a good Christian school located just fifteen minutes from our new home. Christy finished kindergarten there and excitedly looked forward to entering first grade in the fall. When September 1981 arrived, however, the adjustment from kindergarten to first grade was more difficult than either Christy or I had anticipated. She was now gone from morning until late afternoon, and I found that my time with her was growing shorter and shorter. I began to relish the fifteen-minute drives to and from school, when I could actually spend some time talking with my oldest daughter. I was continually amazed at how bright and articulate she was becoming, and I envied her teachers the time they were able to spend investing in my little girl.

It would have been easier for me to dismiss my own feelings, had Christy been more excited about attending school. As it was, she would sometimes cry and ask to stay home with her two sisters and me. On many mornings it became a difficult struggle to get her out the door and into the car, made worse by the fact that I would have preferred to let her stay home myself. There were a few mornings when I gave in to that impulse and let her stay home, but Mike soon put a stop to that. "She has to go to school, Vickie," he would tell me firmly. "There just isn't any other way."

Of course there was no other way. At the time, home schooling was unheard of. So 1981 became 1982, and our daily routine remained unaltered. At least, the particulars remained unaltered: get up, drive Christy to school, care for the two youngest, pick Christy up, make dinner, clean up, go to bed. However, little by little, I did notice a change—and not for the better. Where Christy had formerly been respectful and obedient, she now began to challenge authority. Where she had cared first and foremost about what Mom and Dad thought, she now was becoming flippant and arrogant, giving more weight to the opinions of her fellow six-year-olds. Even in her academics, the one area in which I would naturally expect progress, she became more sloppy and careless.

My concern about Christy's schooling increased. I could no longer confidently tell myself, "It may be hard on me, but we're doing what's best for her." Since starting first grade, she had lost much of her former obedience, respectfulness, and love for learning. Was it best for her?

All this is not to say that Christy was attending a bad school. She had a wonderful teacher, and her school had a reputation for excellent academics. In fact, it was not the negative aspect of her education that finally convinced me something had to change. Rather, it was the strong conviction that I was neglecting my God-given responsibilities.

It happened one afternoon after Christy came home from school. As I fixed dinner, she told me about the excitement of the day. Christy was particularly enthusiastic about the Bible memorization her class was working on. She recited the verse she had learned, and told me how her teacher had explained its meaning. I suddenly stopped what I was doing and looked at her, overwhelmed by an unaccountable sense of jealousy. "Yes, it's wonderful that her school teaches the Bible," I thought to myself, "But...that's my job!" I remembered some verses I had run into just that week in the book of Deuteronomy, which had really made an impression on me:

> Hear, O Israel! The Lord is our God, the Lord is one! And you shall love the Lord your God with all your heart and with all your soul and with all your might. And these words, which I am commanding you today, shall be on your heart; and you shall teach them diligently to your sons and

shall talk of them when you sit in your house and
when you walk by the way and when you lie down
and when you rise up. (Deuteronomy 6:4-7)

I was hit by the conviction that Mike and I should be
the ones teaching spiritual truths to our children. God
had given us the responsibility to train them, and apparently we were to be doing this in the various situations
that would arise throughout the course of each day. But
how could we do this if our children were gone to school
five days a week? Besides, much of what they would
learn in school might have to be unlearned at home if we
were to succeed at the task of teaching godliness.

It was during this crucial period that I turned on
Christian radio one day and heard about home schooling. As dissatisfied as I was, this broadcast of Focus on
the Family with Dr. James Dobson came to me like good
tidings from a distant land: fathers and mothers teaching their own children! It wasn't that the idea itself was
astounding to me; in fact, I had been subconsciously
entertaining it for weeks. The really earth-shattering
news was that real families were actually doing it. It was
possible. However, as enthusiastic as I was about this
new concept of home education, I hesitated to mention
it to Mike. After all, whenever I had an impulse to keep
Christy home, it was always Mike who insisted on her
attending school. I resolved to take the situation to the
Lord—and quietly bide my time.

The Lord was not long in acting. In 1982, Mike's legal
career had already taken a turn toward constitutional
issues, especially religious freedom cases. In addition to

working part-time as the General Counsel for Beverly LaHaye's Concerned Women for America, he was also running his own advocacy organization, the Bill of Rights Legal Foundation. Near the end of the 1982 school year, Mike flew to Utah to talk about religious liberty on the LaHayes' television show. He was not the only guest on the show that day. Appearing immediately after him was Dr. Raymond Moore, one of the earliest advocates of home schooling.

While waiting together to appear on the program, the two guests struck up a conversation. Dr. Moore had not talked very long before he had Mike completely sold on the idea of home education. I remember Mike coming home that night and announcing, "Vickie, I want to consider teaching our kids at home." God knew exactly what He was doing in the way He brought both Mike and me around to the idea of home education. Mike is one of the most impulsive people I know. He can see a new idea and say, "This looks great; I'm going for it." I, on the other hand, have been known to debate for thirty minutes about which dress to wear! A major decision, like how to educate my children, can take me months of thought and prayer.

Throughout the school year, God had been preparing me for Mike's quick decision to home school. Had the concept been a completely foreign one at the time Mike came home and made his announcement, my reaction would probably have been borderline panic. As it was, I was elated. This was exactly what I had been waiting for.

Although missing Christy during the day helped to emotionally prepare me for our decision to home school, it was not the foundational reason for that decision. Mike and I decided to home school our children primarily because we felt it was a matter of obedience to God. We spent many hours considering both the command to diligently instruct our children in God's Word, and the method God prescribes for this spiritual training. We came to the conclusion that we could not follow this plan of spiritual instruction if our children were away from home for the majority of the day. However, if we were going to keep our children home throughout the course of the day, that meant we needed to personally provide their academic instruction as well as their spiritual instruction.

Scripture, as I read it, does not explicitly command parents to teach their children academics. There is no verse saying, "Thou shalt teach thy children geometry." However, Mike and I feel that teaching our children academics is the best way (and for us, the only way) to obey God's command to teach our children to love God and His law.

We have seen many benefits from our decision to home school: academic excellence, godly children, and remarkable family closeness, just to name a few. These, we feel, are directly due to the fact that God's methods produce supernatural results. However, they are not our foundational reason for home schooling. We continue to home school even when we see no benefits whatsoever, because our foundation is based on the unchanging Word of God.

It was this point that Mike gently drove home to me that day, many years ago, when I was tempted to quit home schooling. "We're not doing this to gain certain results, or to achieve some human goal," he reminded me. "We're doing this out of obedience to God." Needless to say, we did not quit home schooling. I simply readjusted my thinking and placed my trust back in God, not myself.

Neither Mike nor I believe that all Christians (or even all home schoolers) must adopt our personal interpretation of Scripture. I shared our interpretation of the Deuteronomy passage with you more as a part of our own story than as an argument for others to choose home education. Your own biblical basis for home schooling may be found in any (or all) of the books in the Bible. However, I do encourage all mothers and fathers to thoroughly consider their children's education in light of Scripture, become convinced in their own minds as to God's direction for their families, and act accordingly.

WHY IS A BIBLICAL FOUNDATION SO IMPORTANT?

Jesus told a story to illustrate the importance of having a solid foundation. There were two men, he said, who both set out to build houses for themselves. One chose his location carefully and set to work building his home on a rock. It was a bit lonely, perhaps, and none too warm—but it was solid. The other man chose a lovely spot with an excellent view of the sea, even if the terrain was rather sandy. Each man finished his construction project and settled down in his new home.

Then the storm came. The man whose house was built on a rock sat listening as the wind whipped around the sides of his house and whistled through distant trees.

Rain came down in huge splashes, followed by the rhythmic clatter of hailstones. Lightning lit up the black sky, followed instantaneously by a crash of thunder. The house shuddered—but stood firm.

Meanwhile, down in the sandy valley, the second man huddled in one corner of his swaying home and tried to block his ears to the sound of the wind. Suddenly, the house buckled—the sand beneath had given way. The man scrambled outside just as his house caved in and crashed into a heap on the sand. He found shelter from the hailstones some distance away, and watched as the wind blew away the rubble that had been his home.

Each man's foundation was tested when the storm came. In the midst of rain, hail, and wind, only the structure with a solid foundation could stand.

This story's application in my own life is rather obvious—a solid, scriptural foundation is absolutely necessary to make it through the difficult days. I need a firm foundation as I set out on this project of "building" godly children. Like the houses in the story, my time of testing will be when the storms come: days when we are way off schedule, the kids are fighting, the phone is ringing off the hook, and nothing seems to be going as I want it to.

Unlike a literal building, however, I can easily stray from my foundation. When I am getting frustrated with my children, it seems so much easier just to crash than to stand firm. That's when I have to take some very practical measures to place myself firmly on the rock of God's Word.

Several years ago, we had a certain framed print hanging on our living room wall. It depicted a mother goose leading her five little goslings through a gateway. Inscribed below the picture was a saying that read: "God will always give you the strength to follow where He leads you." On one particularly "stormy" school day, I was frazzled to the point of explosion. I had been struggling to motivate one of my children to finish her literature composition, the toddler was constantly demanding my attention, and the house was a complete disaster. I remember walking into the living room and just standing there looking at that picture, praying for God to give me the strength to keep going. I knew He wanted me to be home schooling my children, but I just needed the reminder that He would enable me to carry out His will. That picture in the living room pointed me back to my foundation on many occasions.

I also keep verses posted around the house to help me stay focused throughout the day. Just above our kitchen sink (what mother doesn't spend quantity time there?) is a small plaque inscribed with the words of Zechariah 4:6, "Not by might nor by power, but by my Spirit," says the Lord of hosts. I can't tell you how many times I have been washing dishes, listening to the noise of my children, and feeling that there was absolutely no power left in me—only to be reminded that my work needs to be accomplished by the Spirit of God.

Sentence prayers have also been a way for me to "tap into" God's strength throughout the day. Even when I don't feel I can go somewhere to pray and collect my thoughts, I can always send up a quick prayer to God. "Give me patience, Lord!" "Show me how to help these kids love each other." "I need wisdom." "I'm losing it—help me be a good example!"

Even our regular school schedule can serve as a means of pointing me back to my true foundation. We always start the school day with a flag salute, followed by a short time of Bible reading and prayer. Each child has an assigned day for selecting a passage of Scripture and reading it aloud for the rest of us. I am often blessed to hear the Bible verses that my children choose, and it sets a good tone for the entire school day.

Finding practical ways to weave Scripture and prayer into the school day has truly been a lifesaver for me. We mothers are all too human, and we can often forget the big picture when the small details overwhelm us. That's why I have had to keep myself reminded of the most important things by the simple force of habit.

Circumstances change. Enthusiasm waxes and wanes. Results come and go. God and His Word, however, remain constant. "Forever, O Lord, Thy word is settled in heaven," the psalmist writes in Psalm 119:89. The apostle Paul tells us that "If we are faithless, he remains faithful; for He cannot deny Himself" (2 Timothy 2:13). The Word of God is a firm foundation that we can stand upon even when the rest of life seems chaotic. I would encourage each home schooling mother to find the basis for what she is doing, and to stand firmly upon it.

As you seek to find your own ways to turn to God throughout the school day, remember that you aren't alone, nor are you doing this in your own strength. God wants you to rely on Him even more than you do. He is faithful to be found by those who seek Him.

WHAT IF MY HUSBAND DOESN'T SHARE MY CONVICTION?

A few years ago, I traveled with Mike to a state home school convention, to speak on the practicalities of home schooling a large family. While public speaking is certainly not my favorite thing to do, I do greatly enjoy the opportunity for one-on-one interaction with other home schooling moms. After one of my speeches, I stood in the convention hall, talking with several of these mothers. During a lull in conversation, one woman approached me.

"Are you Mrs. Farris?" she asked. When I answered that I was, she proceeded to shake my hand. "You are such a lucky woman," she told me. "I'm envious when I see how supportive your husband is of your home schooling. I really had to twist my husband's arm just to get him to allow me to home school my children. He's really not enthusiastic about it at all, and I feel so alone in what I'm doing."

There are many women whose situations resemble that of this lonely mother. These women feel that they are in this alone. Some of their husbands are non-Christians who do not understand their wives' convictions about home education; some are Christians who simply don't like the idea of their wives teaching their children. What is a woman in this situation to do? What is the proper way for her to walk in obedience to the Lord?

There are two categories of unsupportive husbands: those who are unenthusiastic about home schooling but willing to let their wives try it, and those who forbid their wives to home school outright. If your husband is one of the former, I would encourage you to obey God in what you feel He has called you to do. I would strongly recommend that you surround yourself with other mothers from a local church or home school group who can help support you and keep your eyes focused on the Lord. For those in areas where home schoolers are scarce, there is an ever-growing number of online support groups and communities. Support from like-minded people is vital for every home schooling mom, especially those who are unsupported by their husbands.

Despite the importance of human support, however, your primary source of spiritual support for your home schooling will have to be the Lord. Our human husbands and friends can never be there for us every second of the day, but the Lord can. Women with and without supportive husbands alike need to rely on the continual presence of the Holy Spirit to show them new truths and remind them of old ones. No Christian home schooling mother is truly alone.

The second category of unsupportive husband, however, requires a different approach. If your husband clearly does not want you to home school even after you have respectfully appealed, God's instruction for you is clear: "Wives, be subject to your own husbands, as to the Lord" (Ephesians 5:22). The apostle Peter emphasized that this command applies to wives of unbelievers as well as to those of believers: "In the same way, you wives, be submissive to your own husbands so that even if any *of them* are disobedient to the word, they may be won without a word by the behavior of their wives, as they observe your chaste and respectful behavior" (1 Peter 3:1-2).

I can think of few things more difficult for a mother than doing something she believes is not God's best for her children. If you are in this situation, be comforted that God rewards those who obey Him. I believe that home education has been successful for this very reason—it is God's way, and God's ways work. However, for mothers whose husbands have forbidden them to home school, God's way is to submit to your husband. Just as we home schooling mothers need to obey God and trust Him with the results, so you, in obeying God by obeying your husband, can trust Him to take care of your children.

For those of us who do have supportive husbands, we should not fail to thank God for this tremendous blessing. Such husbands can certainly play a key role in helping us to remember just why we are doing what we are doing. As my earlier story illustrates, there were several days when I might have quit home schooling were it not for Mike's support and encouragement. If you have a husband who is 100 percent enthusiastic about your home schooling, let him help you as you seek to remember your foundation on a daily basis.

BE STRONG AND COURAGEOUS

"Hi Vickie, it's me," said the voice on the other end of the telephone line. I immediately recognized her as one of my friends from church, the mother of several young children. Her oldest child was just approaching school age.

"I was wondering if you had a few minutes to talk to me about home schooling. Basically, I'm convinced that it's God's best...but I'm still worried about how I would actually do it. I have all these little ones around the house, and I just don't know how to handle them while I'm trying to teach. And I just wonder about my own abilities, and whether or not I'll make a good teacher."

These worries were certainly familiar to my ears. I have probably heard almost every fear or worry that could keep a mother from home schooling. In addition to the worries expressed to me by this particular young mother, I have heard such fears as: "I don't know if I'm patient or organized enough." Or: "Will I get enough time for myself?" Others worry: "How will I teach my kids a foreign language? What will I do when they reach high school?" And, perhaps the most common fear of all: "Do I really know what I'm doing? I've never been trained as a teacher. How can I expect to do a good job with my kids?"

These fears can be very real for many mothers, and they are worth addressing. In fact, I would like to spend some time in the following chapters addressing these more practical aspects of home schooling. However, my main focus at this time is whether or not we should be fearful about doing something that God has commanded us to do.

When I see fear and hesitation on the part of women who are otherwise convinced that home schooling is God's plan for them, I am always reminded of the children of Israel as they were preparing to enter the Promised Land for the first time. Despite all they knew of the Lord's power and might, and despite God's clear instruction to enter the Promised Land and conquer it, they balked. When their spies came back and reported that Canaan was inhabited by warriors and giants, the Israelites lost their courage. They should have known that God had the power to help them carry out His plan, but instead they were overcome by fear. As punishment, all but the two spies who trusted God were forbidden from entering the Promised Land. (See Numbers 13-14.)

Forty years later, after that faithless generation had passed away, their children again stood at the edge of Canaan preparing to enter. At that time, God had a very specific message for His people:

> "Be strong and courageous, for you shall give this people possession of the land which I swore to their fathers to give them. Only be strong and very courageous, to be careful to do according to all the law which Moses My servant commanded you; do not turn from it to the right or to the left, so that you may have success wherever you go. This book of the law shall not depart from your mouth, but you shall meditate on it day and night, so that you may be careful to do according to all that is written in it; for then you will make your way prosperous, and then you will have success. Have I not commanded you? Be strong and courageous! Do not tremble or be dismayed, for the Lord your God is with you wherever you go." (Joshua 1:6-9)

The Israelites had a formidable task ahead of them. (If you think raising and home schooling a large family is difficult, try conquering the inhabitants of Canaan!)

God, in exhorting the Israelites to be courageous, simply asked them, "Have I not commanded you?" This should be reason enough for any of us to be courageous.

God has given each of us a difficult job to do. When I feel the task before me is particularly impossible, I love to read the above passage as if it were written directly to me. We need to remember God's commands—the specific foundation for our individual decisions to home school. We need to keep His Word in the forefront of our minds and "meditate on it day and night." And then, knowing that God is with us, we should obey Him.

Be strong and courageous—with God's strength, you can do it! If God has commanded us to perform a certain task, He will provide the strength, the ability, and the means.

When we are confident that He wants us to do something, we can be sure that He will enable us to obey Him. "For it is God who is at work in you, both to will and to work for His good pleasure," Paul tells us in Philippians 2:13. Are you convinced that, by home schooling, you are working for God's good pleasure? If not, you need to take the time to study Scripture and arrive at such a conclusion—for "each one of us shall give account of himself to God" (Romans 14:12). If, however, you are convinced that home schooling is God's purpose for your family, take God at His word. He will work in you to accomplish the job He has given you.

As the nation of Israel finally prepared to enter Canaan under Joshua's leadership, God required of them one final test of faith. He commanded the priests carrying the Ark of the Covenant to lead the people across the Jordan River. But there was a catch: the priests had to step into the flooded river first, before God would part the waters.

As the people watched the Levite priests approaching the swollen Jordan, perhaps they wondered just how they were going to cross. However, as soon as the priests demonstrated their obedience by stepping into the water, the river waters were stopped up in a heap, creating a path for the entire nation into the Promised Land. Israel's job was simply to remember why they were crossing into Canaan: because God had commanded them to do it. God's job was to provide the way.

So it is with us. I have spoken with so many mothers who were, figuratively, standing on the banks of the Jordan and wondering how to cross. They knew what God's command was. They had seen His great strength and power. And yet they hesitated to take that step of faith into the river. I urge such women to "be strong and very courageous." Remember the why, and God will take care of the how.

"The Lord is the one who goes ahead of you; He will be with you. He will not fail you or forsake you. Do not fear, or be dismayed" (Deuteronomy 31:8).

Trust in the Lord with all thine heart; and lean not unto thine own understanding. In all thy ways acknowledge him, and he shall direct thy paths.

PROVERBS 3:5-6, KJV

3

A MATTER
OF SURRENDER

*Learning to Trust God
with My Family Size*

L ord, you couldn't possibly want us to stop using
birth control, could you?!" The idea was absolutely
preposterous! How irresponsible! How totally against
what we had been taught! And how very, very scary! And
yet the thought persisted.

We were almost at the end of our first year of home
schooling, which had gone well. I was challenged by my
new role as "teacher," in addition to the extra managing
that was necessary to balance homemaking and teaching.

But God encouraged us in many ways, not the least of which were the positive comments from both sets of grandparents, who had originally been very doubtful about our decision to home school. I was also very happy to have Christy home again, and she was enjoying it as well.

By the time we finished our first year of home schooling, Christy was seven, Jayme was five, and Katie was two and a half. I did have thoughts of perhaps having another child some time within the next several years, but at the time I was very glad not to be pregnant. I loved being a mother and having babies, but I hated being pregnant. I had nausea that lasted the full nine months of pregnancy—severe at first, dropping to moderate during the last five months or so. My nose always stuffed up—"rhinitis of pregnancy" they called it—and of course I didn't particularly like being fat and uncomfortable.

Mike was actually perfectly content with our three little girls. I had a strong desire from the very beginning to have a little boy, and I was willing to try again for a little Michael junior. Mike, however, felt that we already had our hands full, and he was really enjoying the girls. Whenever I mentioned the possibility of another child, he expressed doubts about being able to handle another baby and another pregnancy.

I would have been very content to bide my time, continuing to use birth control while merely entertaining the possibility of another child sometime in the future. However, a few nagging thoughts, along with a series of minor but very important events, combined to start leading me in a whole new direction.

The first of those events occurred in 1978, between the births of Jayme and Katie, when we lived in Spokane, Washington. I remember riding in the car with Mike past Manito Park on the South Hill of Spokane, engrossed in an article about abortion written by C. Everett Koop. "Listen to this," I suddenly said to Mike. "This article says that birth control pills and IUDs can act as abortifacients, preventing a fertilized egg from implanting into the uterus!" Both of us were truly astounded. By then we both had very strong convictions against abortion, but we had also been using an IUD as our method of birth control. In fact, two weeks after I had had my IUD removed in the hopes of having a second child, we had learned that I was already six weeks pregnant! My doctor had been amazed—he had actually called it a "miracle"—that the pregnancy had survived the removal of the IUD. Unknown to us at the time, God had been extremely merciful to us in our ignorance and had preserved the life of our second daughter Jayme, who was born on October 26, 1977.

Now, as Mike and I rode together through Spokane, we immediately knew we could no longer use an IUD. I had not yet had a new one inserted since Jayme's birth, so we discussed our other options and decided to try a diaphragm.

The significance of this event to me was not so much that we changed our method of birth control, but that this was the first time I began to doubt what I had been taught about birth control. I had never before questioned the use of birth control, and I had certainly never thought of it in connection with abortion. Birth control was the responsible thing for young couples in America to do in order to live within their means and help preserve the planet. Mike had even won a speech contest in college advocating zero population growth, although he had softened his views a bit and was willing to consider three or maybe four children!

I was truly shaken to the core after reading that article by Dr. Koop. Why hadn't anyone ever told us about the possible consequences of using these particular birth control methods? What if I had already unknowingly aborted some of my own children? The thought of that was agonizing and difficult for me to deal with. Only when Mike reminded and assured me of God's grace, forgiveness, and protection—especially in the face of ignorance—was I able to have peace. But I still felt anger at the medical community for what appeared to be deception, or at the very least, partial rather than full disclosure. For the first time I began to realize that what was taught and practiced in the medical community might not be what I could in good conscience follow as a Christian. I realized I needed to think for myself even in medical situations and make sure that everything I did in this area was consistent with Scripture.

Even so, the thought of not using any birth control was so foreign to my thinking that several years passed before I even came close to considering that idea. During those years, I spent many a Sunday morning listening to sermons on varying topics, but they very often had the similar themes of God's sovereign hand in our lives, His goodness and faithfulness to us, and the importance of letting Him be Lord of our lives. "Let go and let God" was a popular phrase among Christians at that time. "Trust and Obey" was the name of an oft-sung hymn, as well as an important teaching.

One of my favorite verses was one that I had learned years before when Mike and I were in The Navigators, a Christian group on the campus of Western Washington State College: "Trust in the LORD with all thine heart; and lean not unto thine own understanding. In all thy ways acknowledge him, and he shall direct thy paths" (Proverbs 3:5-6, KJV).

Mike and I had our third daughter, Katie, on August 31, 1980—a birth we had "planned" by stopping the use of the diaphragm. After Katie's birth, as I mentioned earlier, we were trying to decide whether we would have any more children. With three young daughters already, we were pushing the limits of what was acceptable. As I prayed about what to do, I couldn't help feeling just a little bit hypocritical asking God to reveal His will while we remained in control of the situation. We were basically saying, "Lord, we intend to continue preventing pregnancies unless You show us otherwise or supernaturally intervene."

Now if we really trusted God fully, I began to think—if we really believed that He is the Creator and in charge of the womb, and if we really believed that He is a good God—why not let Him be in charge? If we really want to know what His will is for us, why not let Him show us? Would He give us a child to spite us or allow a new life to form that would harm us?

At this same time, I had a Catholic neighbor who began to talk to me about natural family planning. She and her husband did not use birth control devices; rather, they used a form of abstinence based on a medically tested system of determining the time of ovulation. She gave me a book to read which seemed incredible to me at the time. It was the first natural family planning material I had ever read. I could not believe that someone would actually advocate not using birth control pills or devices. It seemed mighty risky to me. And yet their arguments on taking responsibility for one's actions made a lot of sense.

Artificial birth control, they argued, opens the way for sex without responsibility and wrongly separates pleasure from procreation. They felt that true unity with your partner was not possible with an artificial barrier in the way. Better to abstain during fertile times and come together again in true unity than to have any kind of barrier in place in order to enjoy the pleasures of sex without the natural consequences. Even though this was still a form of birth control, it was revolutionary thinking to me.

Another incident that made a deep impression on me during this period of wrestling and questioning was in the early 1980s. We had moved to Olympia, Washington, two months after Katie was born. An acquaintance of mine who attended our church, Westwood Baptist, became very upset over an unexpected pregnancy. She already had three children, and the pregnancy was definitely an unwanted "accident." Many ladies in the church were praying for her, because she was struggling with depression over the pregnancy and was having a very difficult time accepting her situation. Her pregnancy went smoothly, however, and she gave birth to a little boy.

What made such an impression on me was the incredible testimony she gave during an evening service some time later. She stood up and, through her tears, thanked the Lord for giving her that little son. She told of the struggle she'd had when she was pregnant and then what a tremendous blessing that little boy had been to their whole family since his birth. She publicly thanked the Lord for overriding her own desires and for giving her such a precious gift! If she had had the opportunity to choose what to do, that little boy would never have been born. Consequently, the whole family would have missed a wonderful blessing.

I couldn't help but think of Isaiah 55:8-9, "For My thoughts are not your thoughts, neither are your ways My ways," declares the LORD. "For as the heavens are higher than the earth, so are My ways higher than your ways, and My thoughts than your thoughts." When it comes to decisions regarding human life, how can we trust ourselves to make the right decision? We are very often tempted to decide according to our own selfish desires.

Unexpected blessing, responsibility, trust, true unity, God's faithfulness, "lean not unto thine own understanding"—with all these thoughts swirling in my head, I finally came to the point of asking that preposterous question: "Lord, You couldn't possibly want us to stop using birth control, could You?" And He seemed to whisper back: "Trust Me. Don't trust your own understanding, don't trust what everyone else is doing, don't trust your diaphragm—trust Me."

"But we could have ten children or something!"

"Trust Me."

"But I don't know if I can handle it."

"Trust Me."

"But I might end up big and fat and unattractive!"

"Trust Me."

"Well," I said weakly, "I'll try, but what about Mike?"

Mike was skeptical, to say the least. "I don't know, Vickie, we could end up with ten children or something!" Once again, however, the Lord spoke to Mike's heart very quickly and very decisively, after He had already prepared me over a period of several years. Mike had recently been ordained through our local church in preparation for his new job in Washington, D.C. He was invited to a pastors' seminar taught by Bill Gothard, and one of the things Bill discussed that day was the fact that children are always mentioned in the Bible as unqualified blessings. According to Mike, he did not condemn birth control, but it was obvious that he believed trusting God for one's family size was the pathway to blessing. He encouraged the men at the seminar to have as many children as their faith could handle!

When Mike came home and told me the things Bill had said, we decided then and there, with some trepidation, to trust God and stop using birth control. As an added and much needed bolster to my faith, however, I asked the Lord to do me a favor. I had always gotten pregnant immediately upon removal of any birth control devices (and in fact, as I mentioned earlier, Jayme was conceived with an IUD in place). I asked the Lord to please show me that He truly was in control of the womb—that He could close it as well as open it, and that conceiving was totally in His control and not something that automatically happens. I asked Him to give me one month of not using birth control during which I would not get pregnant. That would be enough to convince me that God truly was in control, because I knew from experience that we were extremely fertile.

This was in February 1983. March came and went, and I did not get pregnant, much to my surprise. By the end of April, however, my period was late, and sure enough—I was pregnant! I was not particularly elated about being pregnant, but God had clearly answered my specific request, and I felt certain that we were in God's will. I recorded both my prayer and God's answer to it in my prayer journal, along with these words:

Dear, dear Lord, how wonderful You are! How magnificent! How powerful! How compassionate and understanding!…Lord, Your mighty hand protected us this last month, and it was You alone! Lord, thank You for showing us that You are truly in control of the womb, and You can stop pregnancy as well as initiate it! It's a miracle for us, since I conceive so easily. Thank you for answering my questioning, fearful, doubtful heart. Lord, you're so sweet and dear and wonderful! How can I now do anything but trust You for our family size? Don't let me forget this!

FALTERING STEPS OF FAITH

I was feeling unusually well at the beginning of this fourth pregnancy—I had very little, if any nausea, and I was gaining very little weight. I thought, "Wow! This isn't so bad. Maybe God is being gracious to me because I obeyed His leading." But in the tenth week of the pregnancy, I started spotting, which I had never done in a pregnancy before. When I called the doctor, he said that everything was probably fine—it can be perfectly normal to spot during a pregnancy. But I had an uneasy feeling about it. I went in for a sonogram that Friday, and I'll never forget the little image of the fetus that I was able to see on the sonogram screen. No one told me at the time what the official results of the sonogram indicated, and I was too young and inexperienced to know or to ask. I had to wait until Monday for a call from my doctor.

As I prayed that night, asking the Lord for protection for this little one I was carrying, I went to the Psalms as I often do for comfort and encouragement. I was reading in Psalm 71 when I came to these words in verse 6: "By Thee I have been sustained from my birth; Thou art He who took me from my mother's womb; My praise is continually of Thee." Even though those words are referring to a healthy birth, the Lord used them to speak to me in a different way and to prepare me for what was about to happen. In my heart, I heard His voice saying to me, "I have your little one in My hands. If you lose this child, remember that I am the one who is taking him from your womb. Your child will be safe in My hands— just trust Me."

As I continued to read, I came to verse 20, and the Lord spoke a promise to my heart through these words: "Thou, who hast showed me many troubles and distresses, wilt revive me again, and wilt bring me up again from the depths of the earth." The phrase "depths of the earth" can refer to Sheol or the womb (as in Psalm 139:15), and I strongly felt that the Lord was saying to me, "I will give you another child. I will raise up another little one from your womb."

Early the next morning, as I rose in the dark, I passed some large clots and I'm certain I lost the baby at that point. Later that morning, Mike called a friend of his—a strongly pro-life doctor in Tacoma, Washington—and asked if he would be willing to examine me. We left our three girls with some friends and drove up to Tacoma from Olympia to see the doctor that afternoon. After a thorough examination, he confirmed that I had lost the baby, and he recommended a D&C at a local hospital immediately. Mike and I were totally unprepared for such a decision, but we both had confidence in the doctor, and we decided to trust his judgment.

Soon I found myself being prepared for surgery in the labor and delivery section of the hospital. I could hear a woman giving birth and the cry of her newborn baby as I was being wheeled into a nearby room to have the remains of my baby removed. I'll never forget that moment and how heartless everyone seemed. As I lay crying and snuffling on the operating table, the anesthesiologist asked me if I had a cold. No one said any kind words to me or expressed any kind of compassion for my situation. All I had to cling to was God and His Word, but I was struggling with that, too. Why had God allowed this to happen, just when we had purposed to obey Him?

The months following the miscarriage were difficult and sometimes painful. In fact, the Monday after my surgery, my original doctor called to say, "Mrs. Farris, everything looked okay on the sonogram. I think you're just not as far along as we thought." I had to tell him I had miscarried early Saturday morning and had a D&C done by our friend. His call was very ironic and renewed the pain.

Every time I saw someone with a baby or even walked by the infant clothing area in a department store, I had to fight back tears. I cried out to the Lord during this time, asking Him to help me trust Him and deal with the pain. He gave me two special verses that I clung to: Job 1:21 and Jeremiah 29:11. In Job 1:21, Job spoke these words after he lost all his possessions: "Naked I came from my mother's womb, and naked I shall return there. The LORD gave and the LORD has taken away. Blessed be the name of the LORD." I prayed for such an attitude!

The Lord also encouraged me greatly with Jeremiah 29:11, "'For I know the plans that I have for you,' declares the LORD, 'plans for welfare and not for calamity to give you a future and a hope.'" That verse, along with the promise God had given to me the night before I miscarried, truly did keep me hopeful. It also helped me to trust the Lord even when it seemed that He had dealt me a pretty low blow.

Despite the difficulty, however, I soon began to see some things that God was doing in all of this. My attitude about getting pregnant had certainly changed dramatically. Whereas before I had been resigned to the very likely possibility of it, now I desperately wanted to be pregnant and was not about to take it for granted. God also impressed upon me the fact that He truly was in control of the womb, not only for conception but for an entire pregnancy. A healthy pregnancy was truly a gift, which God could withdraw at any time if He chose to do so. A healthy baby was a very precious reward from the Creator Himself—a reward that we should indeed accept with great humility and appreciation.

Impatiently, I followed my doctor's instructions to wait three months before trying to get pregnant again. We dutifully went back on birth control, and when the three months were completed I anxiously waited to see what would happen. Several months went by and nothing happened. I began to wonder and worry—"Oh no!" I thought. "Maybe I'm too old now, and I won't be able to have any more babies!" (I was 33 at the time.) I finally conceived in early February, and Jessica Danielle was born November 1, 1984.

Jessica was a beautiful baby and a true delight to us all, but when my periods returned a year later, I was shocked and dismayed. Until then, nursing had always indefinitely held off my periods and the ensuing return to fertility. I had planned to nurse Jessica until she was at least two years old, thus giving myself a good two years before getting pregnant again. Now what was I going to do? God was not finished with me yet in this area of my life!

Even though I wanted to obey God and trust Him for our family size, I still wanted to control the timing and spacing of those little blessings! My plans to use nursing to maintain the spacing I wanted were falling apart, but I was not ready to get pregnant again after only twelve months. What was God thinking, anyway? Surely He didn't expect me to do that!

After all the Lord had been showing me in past years, and despite what I wrote in my journal about trusting God from then on, Mike and I started using birth control again! I was responding exactly like the Israelites so often did in the Old Testament. God would command obedience and trust, often performing great miracles to encourage and help His people along the way. The people, in turn, would follow Him up to a point. But when the going got tough, they would often lose courage and choose their own way instead. That's exactly what I did, and Mike came right along with me. He had not been having the strong feelings that I had been having about children and birth control, and he had no qualms about using it again. We went for several months like that, and I quickly suppressed any feelings of guilt that cropped up from time to time. I simply did not think I could handle getting pregnant again so soon.

Shortly after we moved to Great Falls, Virginia, two months after I miscarried, I met a woman named Linda Parker at the church we had begun attending. I immediately noticed her because she was very pregnant with her fourth child, which was due close to the time our fourth child would have been due. Linda also had three daughters close in age to our three girls, and over the next year or so we got to know one another and often got together so our girls could play. We discovered that we were both at a similar point in thinking about birth control—we wondered whether it truly was wrong to use it, but we were not ready to stop it completely.

Then one day Linda called me. "Vickie, I've been reading this book that my sister gave me. It gives some really good reasons for not using birth control—you've got to read it!"

"Linda," I said, "I don't think I really want to read that right now. I'll take a look at it some time, but not right now!"

But Linda was persistent. Every time I talked to her, she insisted that I read this book. "I really want to know what you think. It really makes a lot of sense."

Ugh! I did not want to be convicted to stop using birth control again, but I finally gave in to Linda's requests. She gave me the book *The Way Home* by Mary Pride, and I started to read it. Many things in the book began to prick my conscience, but the connection Mary Pride drew between abortion and birth control in chapter 6 was what really knocked me to my knees:

> Family planning is the mother of abortion. A generation had to be indoctrinated in the ideal of planning children around personal convenience before abortion could become popular. We Christians raise an outcry against abortion today, and rightly so. But the reason we have to fight those battles today is because we lost them thirty years ago. Once couples began to look upon children as creatures of their own making,

who they could plan into their lives as they chose
or not, all reverence for human life was lost.
Children as God's gifts whom we humbly receive
are one thing; children as articles of our own
manufacturing are another. You can do anything
you like with what you yourself have made.

Wow! Those were strong words, but they had the
ring of truth about them. I remember crouching on the
floor after I read those words, crying and asking God to
forgive me for my selfishness and disobedience to what
He had been showing me. I hated the plague of abortion
that had come upon our country, and I felt that the very
attitudes I had been harboring contributed in their own
small way to the abortion environment. I determined to
once again "trust and obey" the Lord and "lean not unto
my own understanding." If the Lord thought I could
handle another child—or several more children—then
so be it!

I went to Mike and told him I had read a book that
had reconvicted me about the use of birth control. I
asked him to read portions of the book that I felt were
particularly convicting, and he somewhat reluctantly
agreed. After discussing what we had read together, Mike
and I stopped using birth control for the second time.
(We had only used it about three months—the Lord
worked quickly on us this time!)

Surprisingly enough, it actually took several months
before I was once again pregnant. For my first nine
babies, there were only two times where there was any

real delay—the two babies which followed this miscarriage. And God used the timing of each of these babies to minister comfort to my heart.

If you have ever had a miscarriage, you know that the due date for the lost baby becomes a special and very sensitive date. My lost baby was due in February. The next baby, Jessica, was conceived that same February. And the following baby, Angie Michelle, was born February 3, 1987. Some will think this is a coincidence. But God used this emphasis on February to make me feel He had given us a "double portion" back for the child we had lost. I will always consider His timing a very precious and special gift from our loving Heavenly Father.

After the birth of Angie, I figured I'd have at least a year before I might get pregnant. Wrong again! After nine months my period returned. "You've got to be kidding!" I thought. I remember crying and praying in the shower that night. "Lord, I really don't want to get pregnant so soon again. The thought of it is not pleasant at all—but the thought of disobeying You is even worse!" I just couldn't do it—I couldn't turn away from the Lord again. "Lord, just help me to trust You and give me the strength I need!"

I got pregnant the very next month, and on August 25, 1988, Michael Paul Farris, Jr., was born. He was our first son after five daughters—a wonderful surprise and a special blessing we would have certainly missed if I had had my own way. "Aren't you glad now that you decided to trust me?" the Lord asked, and my heart responded with a resounding "Yes!"

Fruitful Years

I never wrestled again with the Lord over the issue of birth control. While Mike continued to struggle with the thought of no protection and the potential of several more babies, whenever the point of decision came (and we discussed this issue after each new baby was born), Mike always ended up agreeing with me. "Humanly speaking, I find this very hard to do, but my spirit says that you're right," was what he always concluded.

I was actually beginning to get used to the idea of having babies every twenty months or so. When I got pregnant 11 months after Michael was born, I was excited about the possibility of a little brother for Michael. I even thought the Lord was telling me this would be another boy. Just before I found out I was pregnant, I had been reading in Genesis chapter 18, and the words in verse 10 jumped out at me: "This time next year,...[you] shall have a son." I remembered those words when I learned I was pregnant, and I clung to the hope that the Lord indeed had meant those words as a promise to me.

I was so certain we would have another little boy, and that baby inside me was so active, that I reacted in disbelief when our midwife announced, on the morning of May 16, 1990, "It's a girl!"

"Are you sure?" I asked, not wanting to believe it.

"Oh yes, I'm sure," she announced cheerfully.

You would think after all the Lord had been doing to show His faithfulness in this area of my life, I would be able to trust Him completely and be at peace regarding what He chose for me. But no, once again—like the Israelites—I griped and complained in my heart about what the Lord had done. It wasn't enough to have a beautiful, healthy little baby—I wanted another boy! I knew I was wrong to be feeling this way, and I struggled to be content, but after almost two weeks I was still having trouble.

Then something happened to permanently change my perspective. Mike had been speaking at a home school conference, and he came home with a very special gift for me.

"Vickie, you have to look at this," he said, "and be sure to read the note written in the back."

Mike handed me a Bible—a lovely red picture Bible published by David C. Cook and on the very front page it said: "To Emily Anne Farris – Love, L'amb – June, 1990." I flipped to the very back, and on the last page was written this note:

Dear Emily Anne,
You don't know me, but, hopefully, some day we'll meet. You and I would have been born in the same month, but our heavenly Father had different plans for us. He sent me as an ambassador to Earth for only a short while, so I won't be needing His special "handbook for living." Emily, it seems He sent you here for a little while longer, so here's my copy. May the Holy Spirit use it to lead you to righteousness, peace, and joy as you serve as His ambassador here on Earth.

Whenever you see a lamb, remember me and know that my earthly family is praying for you!! In Christ's service,

Lil Ambassador Codington (L'amb, for short)
Isaiah 40:11; 2 Corinthians 5:20-21

The note was written by a precious home schooling mom, Susan Codington, on behalf of the baby she had recently miscarried. The Codingtons had bought the little red Bible for their baby. They chose to give this very special Bible to Emily when they lost their own little one, and I was immediately humbled and honored to receive such a precious gift.

I sat there in our bedroom, reading Susan's note over and over again. The Lord spoke quietly to my heart, "And you were complaining about not having a boy? You need to be thankful for this precious little girl I've given you. Do you understand now? Emily was no mistake—I preserved her life in the womb and I have special plans for her. Who are you to question the Creator?" With a lump in my throat, I asked the Lord to forgive me for my ungrateful and arrogant attitude. And spunky little Emily has been a delight to us now for nine years.

After the birth of Emily, Mike was having a particularly hard time saying yes to another baby. I had not had my "warning" period yet, so we thought we were safe. But even as Mike wrestled with the idea of using birth control again, the Lord made the decision for us. For the first time ever, I got pregnant with no periods between babies. The Lord did not give us a chance to say no this time!

Jonathan Tyler was born December 30, 1991, and Joseph Daniel came 21 months later on September 27, 1993. Since we totally stopped using birth control, we'd had five children in six years. The Lord had completely changed my attitude about getting pregnant. I now looked forward to having a new little person join our family every eighteen months to two years, and I had visions of at least being another "Cheaper by the Dozen" family. I was finally submitted to the Lord in this area of my life—or was I?

Those who hopefully wait for Me will not be put to shame.

ISAIAH **49:23**

4

SURRENDERING AGAIN

Miscarriage, Menopause, and the Rest of My Story

When I got pregnant again just before Joseph's first birthday, I was right on schedule—these two babies would be about twenty months apart. We told everyone right away that number 10 was on the way, and I looked forward to "meeting" this new little person who had begun to grow in my womb. But at my check-up with the midwife, my uterus was not the size it should be for eleven weeks, and the day after my appointment I started to bleed.

When we went to the hospital the following day for a sonogram, I was told that, while an amniotic sac was visible, the baby had probably died several weeks earlier. We decided against an immediate D&C, and I ended up miscarrying completely four days later. The doctor we had dealt with at the hospital advised us to wait at least three months before trying to conceive again. I knew what that meant: birth control!

By this time, the idea of using birth control was repugnant to me—we had not used anything for almost nine years. But Mike felt strongly that we should follow the doctor's advice to allow time for healing. He reasoned that our motive for using it was not ultimately to prevent pregnancy but rather to enhance the chances of conceiving under more healthy conditions. We dutifully went back to using birth control for three months, and then we stopped. The following month I got pregnant, but I miscarried again at about seven weeks. I did not want to resume using birth control this time, and I appealed to Mike, asking that we just trust God to protect us.

I had actually just "happened" to be reading in the book of Ezra and had stumbled upon some verses in chapter 8 in which Ezra refused protection from outside sources in favor of simply trusting God. He was leading a group of Israelites, including children, back to Jerusalem from captivity in Babylon. Instead of requesting a military escort for protection against dangerous marauders and thieves, Ezra chose to ask God for a safe journey in order to maintain a consistent testimony before King Artaxerxes.

Ezra's decision confirmed my own desire to simply trust God for whatever protection we might need in this situation. If Ezra could take that "risk"—especially considering that he had little ones with him—why couldn't we? Mike was willing to try it. Under God's protection, we went another three months without conceiving (interestingly enough, God Himself accomplished exactly what would have happened had we used birth control). In the fourth month, I got pregnant once again. I knew something was wrong, however, when I was not feeling sick by six weeks of pregnancy. Sure enough, I miscarried a third time at six-and-a-half weeks. Needless to say, this was a very difficult time for me. Miscarriages can be very painful emotionally, even when you already have nine children! I was getting mad at God.

"What's going on, Lord? What are You doing to me? Why are You allowing me to get pregnant and get my hopes up, only to snatch away the little ones so quickly? I'd rather not get pregnant at all! I don't know how much more I can take!" I asked the Lord to at least give me a verse to cling to, and He led me to Psalm 25:10, "All the paths of the Lord are lovingkindness and truth to those who keep His covenant and His testimonies."

All the paths of the Lord are lovingkindness? Including three miscarriages in a row? "Okay, Lord, if You say so. I don't understand it, but I choose to believe what you say," I decided.

The Lord then encouraged me tremendously through the September twelfth devotional in Oswald Chambers' *My Utmost for His Highest*. Chambers wrote:

There are times in spiritual life when there is confusion, and it is no way out to say that there ought not to be confusion. It is not a question of right and wrong, but a question of God taking you by a way which in the meantime you do not understand, and it is only by going through the confusion that you will get at what God wants.

Jesus gave the illustration of the man who looked as if he did not care for his friend, and He said that that is how the Heavenly Father will appear to you at times. You will think He is an unkind friend, but remember He is not; the time will come when everything will be explained. There is a cloud on the friendship of the heart, and often even love itself has to wait in pain and tears for the blessing of fuller communion. When God looks completely shrouded, will you hang on in confidence in Him?

Jesus says there are times when your Father will appear as if He were an unnatural father, as if He were callous and indifferent, but remember He is not; I have told you—"Everyone that asketh receiveth." If there is a shadow on the face of the Father just now, hang onto it that He will ultimately give His clear revealing and justify Himself in all that He permitted.

"When the Son of Man cometh, shall He find faith on the earth?" Will He find the faith which banks on Him in spite of the confusion? Stand off in faith believing that what Jesus said is true, though in the meantime you do not understand what God is doing. He has bigger issues at stake than the particular things you ask.

I knew God had a purpose in all of this, and I determined to trust Him and just wait to see what He would do. But, believe me, it wasn't easy! Ever since the first in this streak of miscarriages, the kids and I had been praying every night that the Lord would give us at least one more baby.

I had turned forty just before Jonathan was born, and I was almost forty-two when Joey arrived. Now forty-four, I had been struggling with the very real possibility that I would never be able to conceive and maintain a healthy pregnancy again. I had finally embraced the idea of having a large family with babies coming every couple of years, but now the Lord began asking me a new question: "Are you willing to continue walking with Me in faith, even if you keep losing babies and never give birth again?" It was no longer "How many babies are you willing to accept from Me?" but "How few babies are you willing to accept?"

This whole change in circumstances really caught me off guard. For years and years I was "fertile Fanny," but now I felt like an old, dried-out, dead tree! I went through somewhat of an identity crisis—I was so used to having a baby in my arms that I felt different and strange without one. I realized menopause was not all that far away, and I began to inwardly mourn the waning of my childbearing years.

"Lord, please help me to be fertile spiritually, if not physically!" I cried out. I just didn't like the idea of drying up! Psalm 92:12-15 was (and still is) very encouraging to me: "The righteous man will flourish like the palm tree, he will grow like a cedar in Lebanon. Planted in the house of the Lord, they will flourish in the courts of our God. They will still yield fruit in old age; they shall be full of sap and very green, to declare that the Lord is upright; He is my rock, and there is no unrighteousness in Him."

Mike also reminded me that, even if we had no more babies, I still had years ahead of me as an active home schooling mom. "You're not over the hill yet, Vickie! You've still got young children and many more years of mothering ahead of you." Of course, he was right—but my arms still felt empty!

After that third miscarriage, seven months passed and nothing happened. It was the longest I had ever gone without conceiving. I tried various "remedies" recommended to me by several friends, including progesterone cream and flax oil. Finally, I missed a period, took a home pregnancy test, and yes—a pink line showed up in the little "window."

I was so nervous about the pregnancy that I asked for a sonogram at 6 weeks to make sure everything was okay. As the doctor scanned the screen looking for signs of life, his face held an expression of concern that was not very encouraging. "Mrs. Farris, you appear to have an empty sac here. I just don't see what I should be seeing at this point—but let's wait another week and check this again. Maybe we're just a little early."

I spent the next week praying and asking the Lord to help me keep my eyes on Him, no matter what the outcome of the pregnancy. I asked Him to help me trust in

His goodness and sovereignty and to maintain a proper attitude of submission to His will. When I went to the doctor the following week, Mike came with me.

"Well, Mrs. Farris, we could have good news for you!" the surprised doctor announced. "It's hard to see exactly what's happening, but there is definitely something in there that wasn't there before! Let's take a look at things in another two weeks."

I was greatly encouraged, especially because I was feeling sick to my stomach—the sign of a healthy pregnancy for me. Two weeks later, as I looked at the sonogram screen with the doctor, the "something" had apparently grown, but the doctor did not look happy.

"I don't know—this just doesn't look right," he finally said. "I want to schedule a sonogram for you at the hospital, where the equipment is better and we can hopefully determine what's going on."

When I went to the hospital, my doctor consulted another doctor as they studied yet another sonogram of my womb. "Mrs. Farris, I'm afraid what we're seeing here is arrested growth and the beginnings of a decomposing sac," my doctor explained.

"You're sure the baby is dead, then?" I wanted to know.

"Absolutely. There is no heartbeat, and there is evidence of deterioration around the sac. There is no question in my mind."

After discussing things with Mike, I decided to go along with the doctor's suggestion of a D&C. I did not want to go through another miscarriage like the first one in this series of four, which also occurred at ten-eleven weeks. Also, I had been having some irregular spotting, and a biopsy of my uterine wall taken between this miscarriage and the last one had shown some remaining tissue from previous miscarriages. I wanted to get "cleaned out" and start fresh. I just asked the Lord to protect me in the process.

It was actually a great relief to have the D&C done and be able to move on with my life. This last pregnancy had been such an emotional roller-coaster that I was ready for a break. I actually felt that I could now be very content with the nine healthy children the Lord had given me, and I determined to focus on and be thankful for all that I already had. I no longer felt so driven to have another baby. I just told the Lord I would be content whatever He chose to do, and I believe I finally and truly "let go" of my own desires.

I was not going to use progesterone cream, and I was not going to eat barley green or put any more yucky flax oil on my salads. Although I did not feel there was anything wrong with these remedies, and I knew they had certainly helped other women, I felt that I was putting an improper faith in them rather than in the Lord. If the Lord wanted us to have another baby, I knew He was perfectly capable of doing it all by Himself, without any help from me! If He could bless Sarah with a child in her nineties, He could certainly work with a forty-four year old! And if He chose not to do anything, that was okay, too.

Two-and-a-half months later, as I prepared to fly to Europe for a week with Mike and his parents, I realized my period was slightly overdue. Not being one to have much patience waiting to find out if I'm pregnant, I sent Mike out to buy a pregnancy test the night before we left for Europe. Sure enough, it was positive! Before we left I told our two oldest, Christy and Jayme, and asked them to pray for me.

Our flight to Europe was somewhat of a nightmare—we were delayed for hours and hardly got any sleep. I guzzled coffee to stay awake the next day, and I was finishing off antibiotics and taking decongestants for a sinus infection. For the next four days, I slept very poorly, and I continued to load up on coffee just to keep going. "So much for this pregnancy," I thought wearily. "If this baby survives all this, he's going to have to be tough!"

The night before we left Europe, I remember taking a walk around the huge parking lot of our hotel in Paris, suddenly seized by the fear of yet another miscarriage. "Lord, I don't know if I can go through all this again! I really was at peace about everything—why stir things up one more time, and so soon?"

What came to my mind immediately was 1 Corinthians 10:13, "No temptation [also translated "trial"] has overtaken you but such as is common to man; and God is faithful, who will not allow you to be tempted [tried] beyond what you are able; but with the temptation [trial] will provide the way of escape also, that you may be able to endure it." All I could do was repeat that verse to myself over and over again. Focusing on the fact that God is faithful, and remembering that

He would not allow me to be tempted or tried beyond endurance, was the only thing that brought peace.

On the plane the next day, I thankfully noticed some queasiness for the first time. About a week later, I went once again for a sonogram. My heart was pounding as I drove to the hospital. I had taken a hymnal along with me, and I sang *How Firm a Foundation* as I drove, to calm and encourage myself.

> How firm a foundation, ye saints of the Lord,
> Is laid for your faith in His excellent Word!
> What more can He say than to you He hath said,
> To you who for refuge to Jesus have fled?
>
> "Fear not, I am with thee, O be not dismayed;
> For I am thy God, and will still give thee aid;
> I'll strengthen thee, help thee, and cause thee to stand,
> Upheld by My righteousness, omnipotent hand."
>
> "When through fiery trials thy pathway shall lie,
> My grace, all-sufficient, shall be thy supply;
> The flame shall not hurt thee; I only design
> Thy dross to consume, and thy gold to refine."
>
> "The soul that on Jesus hath leaned for repose,
> I will not, I will not desert to its foes;
> That soul, though all hell should endeavor to shake,
> I'll never, no, never, no, never forsake!"
>
> —George Keith

I walked into the hospital not knowing what to expect, but I was confident that God would somehow see me through whatever lay ahead. As I watched yet another sonogram screen showing the contents of my womb, I actually saw some sort of movement. "What's that little pulsing thing? Is that the heart beating?" I asked hopefully. The technicians looked concerned, and I wanted to know what was going on.

"Oh yes, that's the heart, and it looks fine. We were just wondering what this other shadowy figure was," the technician replied. There was some suggestion of twins, but it was soon determined that this baby had an unusually large umbilical cord.

"Is that something to be concerned about?" I asked.

"We're not sure," came the reply.

Well, oversized cord or not, I had never seen a little heart beating with any of my miscarriages. "Thank You, thank You Jesus!" I whispered.

On my way home from the hospital, I stopped at the HSLDA office and told Christy and Jayme the good news (Mike was out of town at the time). They both squealed and gave me happy hugs. When I told Katie, who had been the least enthusiastic about Mom's having another baby, she actually hugged me and said she was happy and excited for me. "Lord, Your timing is perfect!" I thought.

There was some concern for a while about the baby's cord, but it turned out to be nothing. It seems that when you are forty-five and having your tenth child, you are considered "high-risk," and everyone automatically thinks that something will probably go wrong.

The most disconcerting thing that happened during this pregnancy was a call that came from my doctor around the fifth month. I had decided to go ahead and have an AFP (Alpha-Fetal Protein) blood test taken to check for Down's syndrome and spina bifida, among other things.

"Mrs. Farris," said the voice on the other end of the phone, "I'm afraid I have some bad news. The results of your AFP test have come back, and they show that you've tested positive for Down's syndrome." I was stunned!

"Now, that does not mean that your baby has Down's syndrome for certain," the doctor continued, "but the risk of it is much greater than normal, according to these results. I know that you and Mike would never choose to terminate your pregnancy, but you could have an amniocentesis done to determine the Down's syndrome for sure. It's a risky process, however, and I wouldn't recommend it, considering your convictions."

When I got off the phone, I just sat there, trying to take in and process everything the doctor had said. Katie came into the kitchen just then, upset about something. I responded to her complaining with anger, and she snapped back at me.

"Katie, I can't handle this right now!" I cried. "The doctor just called to tell me our baby probably has Down's syndrome!"

Katie gave me a shocked look. "Oh, I'm sorry, Mom!" she apologized, as I ran off to my room crying.

Later that evening, a lovely little bouquet of flowers sat on the kitchen table for me from Katie. "I love you, Mom, and I'll be praying for you," the card read. It was a very sweet gesture that I will never forget.

When I grilled the doctor about the AFP test at my next visit, I learned some things that helped me feel a bit better. First of all, I learned that this test is often unreliable and results in many false positives. Secondly, the results are read subjectively, as a comparison of women in a similar age group, and this can sometimes skew the results. Finally, even though my readings showed a higher risk than normal, we were still only talking about a 4 percent chance that the baby would have Down's syndrome. I am convinced that this test is often used by the abortion industry to scare women into having the risky amniocentesis procedure performed, as well as sometimes leading them to abort their babies. I would never take this test again unless there was a very good reason for it.

Even though the discussion with my doctor encouraged me, I could just not shake the memory of that initial pronouncement that I tested "positive for Down's syndrome." I knew that if that was what the Lord had chosen for us, it would be a blessing; but it was not something that I actively desired, and it unfortunately remained as a "shadow" hanging over the rest of the pregnancy.

Despite all these forebodings, however, Peter James Farris was born on March 29, 1997—a beautiful, healthy baby boy. He was a wonderful answer to two years of prayer, and the Lord had blessed us against all the odds. I had not used any extra "helps" to get pregnant, I had actually conceived while I was sick and on antibiotics, I used more medication during Peter's pregnancy than any of my other pregnancies, and yet all the predictions of problems had come to naught. Peter was a feisty, active little baby, and he is now the absolute delight of the whole family!

THE POINT OF MY STORY

I have told you the story of our spiritual struggles in the area of family planning for several reasons. First of all, next to inquiries about home schooling, most of the questions I hear from other women concern the issues of birth control, family size, and dealing with miscarriage. Mike jokes that any time he sees me in a lengthy, serious conversation with another woman, he knows that we are probably talking about birth control—and he's usually right!

Secondly, I believe that God has worked in a special way in this area of my life and has taught me many lessons about Himself through our struggle involving birth control. He has shown His faithfulness, His power, His wisdom, His sovereignty, His goodness, gentleness, and mercy. He has increased my faith and deepened my walk with Him in ways I never could have imagined. It is a story that I have been wanting to share for a long time.

Another reason I have spent so much time on this is that I believe issues involving the creation, prevention, and/or destruction of human life are some of the most important issues for each of us to consider and wrestle with today. With abortion flourishing in our country, we need to carefully search our own hearts and examine the attitudes and motives involved in our family planning decisions.

In the context of this book, I wanted you to know exactly why we have so many children, whom we are trying to raise up to be a "godly generation." I wanted you to understand that we did not enter into the "large family thing" lightly. We counted the cost and decided that following the Lord's leading in this area was well worth any difficulty or sacrifice.

I also wanted you to see first-hand the struggles that Mike and I went through as our family grew. We never decided to have a large family *per se*—we merely responded in obedience to God's promptings in our hearts one step at a time. And, as you were able to witness throughout these chapters, our obedience was often very reluctant!

My hope has been to encourage those of you who may be having similar struggles—and I know there are many home schooling moms who struggle with these issues. I've talked to many of you! It is seldom easy to step out in faith, handing over all your decisions to the Lord, and allowing Him to be in total control. It's just plain scary! I think it helps to hear from someone who has faced those same fears and can testify to God's faithfulness.

When I was still thinking through these issues, I would have loved to hear the story of an older woman with many children. How did she feel? Did she ever feel overwhelmed? How did she decide to have a lot of children—or did she consciously decide? How old was she when she had her last child? I longed to talk to someone who had "been there" when I was agonizing over what to do, but for years there was no one.

While I truly hope to encourage those of you who may be struggling as I did, I have an even greater desire to challenge those of you who may not have even thought about birth control as a spiritual issue. In our culture today, the use of birth control is assumed to be the responsible thing to do, and it is not even questioned.

A few weeks ago, I happened to pick up and browse through a little pamphlet that Katie had left in our home during her recent pregnancy. It was published by the American College of Obstetricians and Gynecologists and was given to Katie by her doctor. In the postpartum section of this booklet on pregnancy, under the title "Sex and Birth Control," was this statement: "You can get pregnant even if you are breast-feeding or your periods have not yet started. This means that you need to choose some form of birth control before you have sex for the first time."

"Says who?" was my first thought, and yet this is what young women are told today. Most women would not even consider doing otherwise.

It was not always this way in our country. In the early 1900s, the Comstock Law actually banned the sale and distribution of contraceptive devices in the U.S. This law remained on the books in some states as late as 1961. In the Supreme Court case of *Griswold v. Connecticut*, the dispute concerned the constitutionality of a statute that read:

> Any person who uses any drug, medicinal article or instrument for the purpose of preventing conception shall be fined not less than fifty dollars or imprisoned not less than sixty days nor more than one year or be both fined and imprisoned.

This statute was still a part of the law in Connecticut until 1965!

I was amazed to find out that it was Margaret Sanger who led the pro-birth control movement in the United States. Sanger was arrested several times for opening birth control clinics and advising people on the subject. She also denounced marriage as a "degenerate institution" and sexual modesty as "obscene prudery" in her writings. She herself was very promiscuous, and she at one time openly endorsed the euthanasia, sterilization, abortion, and infanticide programs of Nazi Germany. Margaret Sanger was the founder of the American Birth Control League in this country, which later changed its name to Planned Parenthood.

There are indeed strong ties between birth control and abortion, and that in itself should make us stop and ponder. If we are Christians, we need to search the Scriptures and see what God says on this subject. We need to have a scriptural basis for our decisions in this important area, and not just take the word of The

American College of Obstetricians and Gynecologists! However knowledgeable and wise they may be on other issues, God should certainly be our first authority on the subject of human life.

What Does Scripture Say about Birth Control?

I would like to share with you some things that I found as I searched the Scriptures during my years of questioning and struggle. This is certainly not a full dissertation on the subject, however, and I would encourage you to look into the Word yourself and ask God to show you His truth. My conclusions based on God's Word may not be the same as yours, either, but we must all earnestly seek our answers from Scripture, not the world.

Scriptural Truth #1: God controls the womb. One of the first things I realized from my years of reading Scripture was that God always speaks as though He has an active role in either opening or closing the womb. Indeed, He says to Jeremiah in Jeremiah 1:5, "Before I formed you in the womb I knew you, and before you were born I consecrated you . . ."

David speaks clearly of God's active and continuous involvement in creating life when he says, "For Thou didst form my inward parts; Thou didst weave me in my mother's womb. . . . Thine eyes have seen my unformed substance; And in Thy book they were all written, the days that were ordained for me, when as yet there was not one of them" (Psalm 139:13, 16).

When the patriarch Jacob was tricked into marrying Leah before her sister Rachel, whom Jacob really loved, Genesis 29:31 records, "Now the Lord saw that Leah was unloved, and He opened her womb, but Rachel was barren." When Rachel then complains to Jacob, "Give me children, or else I die," Jacob accurately responds, "Am I in the place of God, who has withheld from you the fruit of the womb?" (30:1-2).

Ruth 4:13 records, "So Boaz took Ruth, and she became his wife, and he went in to her. And the Lord enabled her to conceive, and she gave birth to a son."

According to Scripture, God Himself controls conception—it is never an accident. In fact, Deuteronomy 32:39 tells us plainly, "It is I who put to death and give life." Would God create a life to harm us or to bring trouble and evil into our lives? I believe that is against the very nature of God! So if our Heavenly Father, who loves us deeply, wants to give us the precious gift of human life for good and for blessing, why do we keep saying, "No!"?

Scriptural Truth #2: God highly values fruitfulness. It is very clear from Scripture that God highly values physical fruitfulness, even if we don't. The great covenant that God made with Abraham in Genesis involved fruitfulness. God says to Abraham in Genesis 17:2, "I will establish My covenant between Me and you, and I will multiply you exceedingly." Again in verse 6 He says, "I will make you exceedingly fruitful, and I will make nations of you, and kings shall come forth from you."

Every time God wanted to bless His people, He promised fruitfulness. He told the Israelites in Leviticus 26:9, "So I will turn toward you and make you fruitful and multiply you, and I will confirm my covenant with you." In Deuteronomy 7:13-14, Moses promised the people, "And He will love you and bless you and multiply you; He will also bless the fruit of your womb.... You shall be blessed above all peoples; there shall be no male or female barren among you or among your cattle."

Not only does God highly value fruitfulness—He actually commands it. We see in Genesis 1:28 that the very first command ever given to man was, "Be fruitful and multiply, and fill the earth, and subdue it." I think many people write this off with a "Well, of course God commanded Adam and Eve to be fruitful and multiply—the earth was totally empty!" But as far as I can tell, that command was never revised or revoked, and God's dealings with Adam were always representative of His dealings with all of mankind.

In our culture today, fruitfulness is viewed as a downright curse instead of a blessing. At best, it is considered a pesky nuisance that gets in the way of our fun. People are continually trying to deny and even destroy their own fruitfulness. Unfortunately, many of us Christians have been trained in this way of thinking, and we need to be careful! Scripture clearly places a high value on fruitfulness—are we thinking scripturally as we plan our families, or are we thinking as the world does?

Scriptural Truth #3: God says children are a blessing. Scripture also makes it clear that God considers children to be a blessing and a reward. Psalm 127 and Psalm 128 both speak of the blessings of having children. Psalm 127:3 says, "Behold, children are a gift of the Lord; the fruit of the womb is a reward," and verse 5 adds, "How blessed is the man whose quiver is full of them." In other words, the more children, the better! "Your wife shall be like a fruitful vine, within your house, your children like olive plants around your table. Behold, for thus shall the man be blessed who fears the Lord," declares Psalm 128:3-4.

If we all genuinely believed these verses, I think our birth control pills and devices would go flying out the window, and we would all be hoping and praying for large families. Why don't we see that happening? Perhaps we may think that we can't really serve the Lord the way we should if we are saddled with a large family. I don't see that justification in Scripture, however.

Maybe we think we can't afford a lot of children. But Psalm 37:25 tells us, "I have been young, and now I am old; yet I have not seen the righteous forsaken, or his descendants begging bread." Maybe we know that we won't be able to have or do many things if we have many children. That's called selfishness, and it has no justifiable place in a Christian's life. Maybe we just think we won't be able to handle it, but God says, "Lean not unto thine own understanding." Take God at His word. This is one of the most important applications of that principle. When God says children are a blessing, He really means it, and we need to believe it—despite what the world says, and despite what our hearts may even cry out to us at times. I believe God has a far richer meaning for the word "blessing" (discussed in chapter 12). For now let me mention just one way in which children bless us that is often missed. The reason most people do not want a lot of children is that—let's face it—children are a lot of trouble and a lot of work! They cry, they fight, they mess up the house, they interrupt our sleep and our work, they often need help, patience, forgiveness, and love. In other words, they require us to grow up and shape up, to deny ourselves and to become more like Christ if we are to have any measure of success with them. And what a genuine blessing that is! Children force us onto our knees, drive us to the Lord, and sharpen us for even greater service.

Scriptural Truth #4: Our bodies are not our own. Romans 12:1 says, "I urge you therefore, brethren, by the mercies of God, to present your bodies a living and holy sacrifice, acceptable to God, which is your spiritual service of worship." In addition, Paul continually refers to himself as a "bond-servant of Christ Jesus." A bond-servant literally means "slave," from a word meaning "to bind." The footnote in my Bible says, "The believer who voluntarily takes the position of slave to Christ has no rights or will of his own. He does always and only the will of his Master. For His part, the Lord binds Himself to care for His servant."

If we do choose to become bond-servants to our Lord (and we do have a choice), then our bodies are no longer our own. This flies in the face of the feminists and abortionists who say just the opposite: "Your body is your own, and you hold all right to it." Here again, I believe some of the attitudes we Christians often have toward our own bodies are the very same attitudes that lead some to choose abortion.

The wonderful fact to keep in mind if we struggle with handing our bodies over to the Lord is that, as my Bible notes, "the Lord binds Himself to care for His servant." The "binding" business works both ways, and I find it tremendously encouraging to know that the all-wise God of the universe, who is the embodiment of love, promises to care for and protect me and my body even better than I could do myself!

The Scriptures I have just shared with you are the primary Scriptures the Lord used to speak to my heart over the years concerning the issue of birth control. Of course, there is no verse that says, "Thou shalt not use birth control." However, I believe that the heart of God, as it is overwhelmingly portrayed in Scripture, is one that embraces life, children, and fruitfulness rather than voluntary barrenness.

Although I have obviously developed very strong convictions on this issue over the years, I still firmly believe that decisions concerning birth control must be made between a husband, his wife, and God. I have never told my married daughters that they should not use birth control, or that they would be sinning to do so. I believe the husband should be the final authority on this matter, although I do not think it inappropriate for a wife to appeal to her husband on scriptural grounds. That's exactly what I did, and Mike ended up agreeing with me.

I also feel that in situations where there are medical problems and where a pregnancy may actually be dangerous for the mother, a couple needs to carefully determine what the Lord would have them do. I have seen some wonderful situations where the Lord has blessed couples with children even when the mother had serious medical difficulties, but it is not for me to say that couples should not use birth control in those instances.

We have continued to trust God in this area since Peter was born two-and-a-half years ago. God has been very merciful, and I have had only one very early miscarriage during that time. I truly believe that God knows exactly what He is doing in every single conception He creates. Whether that conception goes on to become a full-term baby or whether it ends in miscarriage, God is in control and His way is always blameless (see Psalm 18:30).

Whether you are struggling to embrace your fertility, with the prospect of a new baby every year; whether you are dealing with the pain of miscarriage and the sense of emptiness and confusion it can bring; or whether you are facing menopause and the likelihood that you will never hold your very own infant in your arms again, you can be sure of this: "Those who trust in the Lord are as Mount Zion, which cannot be moved, but abides forever. As the mountains surround Jerusalem, so the Lord surrounds His people from this time forth and forever" (Psalm 125:1-2).

It is never, ever a foolish thing to entrust yourself into the hands of the living God. His control is much better than birth control. May I urge you to diligently seek the Scriptures and then to "commit your way to the Lord, trust also in Him, and He will do it" (Psalm 37:5).

Blessed be the Lord God, the God of Israel, who alone works wonders.

PSALM 72:18

5

HOME SCHOOLING A HOUSEFUL

The Practicalities of Teaching a Large Family

It was the summer of 1984, and I had just finished the best school year I have ever had in all my years of home schooling because I was able to stay on schedule most of the time. We had few interruptions or outside distractions, we had time to be creative and work on "hands-on" projects, and we had lots of fun in the process!

We had just moved to Virginia in September 1983 so Mike could open up the Washington, D.C. office of Beverly

LaHaye's Concerned Women for America. We were not yet immersed in church activities and responsibilities, and we were still just beginning to build friendships and social connections. We therefore had few outside responsibilities or activities to distract us. Christy (8) and Jayme (6) were enthusiastic about learning and were fun to work with, and Katie was old enough to entertain herself and participate in many of our activities.

Now, however, in the summer of 1984, I was pregnant with our fourth child. We had made our initial decision to stop using birth control, and this was the child God was giving us after my first miscarriage. While I was excited and thankful to be having this child, I was also filled with fear and trepidation concerning the coming school year. "How am I ever going to do this with a new baby?" I wondered. As I looked ahead to our third year of home schooling, the task seemed absolutely impossible. Our baby was due October 31, and I knew that the weeks before the birth would be filled with doctor's appointments and the preparations necessary for a home birth. But it was the period after the baby's birth that really concerned me. "How can I teach when I'm not getting any sleep at night, and I need to be nursing and caring for an infant?" I worried.

I thought I must be crazy to be undertaking such a task, and yet I sensed that this was exactly what God wanted me to do. I was reminded of Abraham, who "by faith…when he was called, obeyed by going out to a place which he was to receive for an inheritance; and he went out, not knowing where he was going" (Hebrews 11:8).

I felt that I, too, did not know exactly where I was going or how I was going to get there, but I knew God was saying, "Go." "Okay, Lord," I thought, "but You're going to have to do this for me, because I cannot see right now how I can possibly handle everything!"

I wish I could remember the many little things the Lord did to help and encourage me that year, but as the year ended I do remember thinking, "We made it! We actually finished our books, the girls learned a lot, and I am still alive and of sound mind! It wasn't as easy as last year, but we made it."

Since then, I cannot tell you how many new school years I have faced with a feeling similar to the trepidation I felt that summer of 1984. "How in the world am I going to do it this year?" I have thought many times, especially during the period when the Lord gave us five children in six years! And yet God has been tremendously faithful, and He has always provided a way for us to complete each school year successfully.

I must admit that we have never had another year like that second year of home schooling, with the relative lack of interruptions and distractions, the enthusiasm of kids and Mom, and the time to be creative. Every year it has gotten more challenging to work out a good schedule, plan our curriculum, and juggle the varying needs of children ranging from toddlers to teens. I have thought back to that 1983-84 school year with much fondness, but I have never, ever regretted our decision to trust God for our family size, despite the resulting challenges in home schooling that decision created.

Psalm 31:8 says, "Thou has set my feet in a large place." God has truly done this for me over the years, not only by giving us a large family, but also by enlarging my abilities and skills in the process. I have been forced to become more organized; I have learned to do things more quickly; I have had to develop a bit more of a drill-sergeant's personality, when my natural tendency is to be merciful and easygoing; and I have had to learn how to focus and concentrate even in the midst of noise and confusion! Indeed, it seems that the Lord has simply increased His grace every time the burden has gotten a little heavier, and He has enabled me to meet each new challenge when it has arisen.

If you have ever wondered how in the world you can teach your children, especially if you have a lot of them, this chapter is for you. I'll share with you a few things we have done to manage the job of teaching our large family, and the next chapter will cover our methods for handling chores and outside activities. As I talk about what has worked for me, I will also share some alternative methods that have worked for other families. Sometimes it just helps to hear how other families are managing their teaching responsibilities, whether it serves to spark some new ideas or just confirm what you are already doing. All of these practical suggestions should be viewed as just that: suggestions. You may take them, leave them, or alter them to fit your own family's individual needs. There is just one point I would like to emphasize, however, before I get into the practical aspects of home schooling a large family.

YES, YOU CAN TEACH!

I recently attended a home school conference held in a large hotel. Because the conference was several days in length, the hotel staff became accustomed to seeing the large families and young children that typify a home school conference. As I was in the hotel deli one night, buying dinner with several of my children, one of the women behind the counter started asking me about home schooling. As usual, one of the first questions she asked was, "So how did you learn how to teach? Do you have a teaching degree?"

I am always a little reluctant to answer this question, because I did earn a college degree in elementary education. Oftentimes the world looks at this fact as the reason for my success in home schooling, and unfortunately many new or prospective home school moms are trapped into that way of thinking as well. "How can I teach my kids if I don't have a teaching degree?" I have been asked on many occasions. "I just don't know what I'm doing!" I believe this is the primary fear that haunts home schooling moms as they consider the task of teaching their own children.

I can honestly say, both to those outside the home school movement and to those inside it, that my B.A. in elementary education did very little to help me in the job of teaching my children at home. In fact, in several ways I believe it hindered me when I first began home schooling. When I attended college in the early '70s, the education establishment was just beginning to overhaul all the "traditional" methods of education. Although at first I was excited by all this "modern" thought, I soon began to doubt its long-term value to me as a teacher.

For example, I entered my college course on children's reading expecting to learn how to teach children to read, or at the very least, how to instill in them an appreciation for reading and literature. Instead, the professor simply assigned us a reading list of children's books. As I sat in my dorm room diligently reading *Sylvester and the Magic Pebble*, I wondered how this "knowledge" would ever be useful to me in the classroom. And in my class on teaching math, again, I expected to gain some knowledge of how to teach addition, subtraction, multiplication, and division at the elementary school level. Instead, my professor just encouraged us to experiment with numbers and find our own numerical patterns. It was interesting, but I could not help doubting its usefulness.

My semester of student teaching proved to be a similar experience. I deliberately chose to student teach under a young teacher in a more "modern" school, hoping to gain some brilliant insight into the educational process. Instead, I left still feeling that I knew nothing about the practical methods of teaching and doubting that many of the young professional teachers of the day knew much more than I did.

It was from this background that I approached the task of teaching my own daughter in 1982. As new as the idea of home schooling was back then, I was convinced that I could do it. I had seen firsthand the futility of the modern educational system, and I was confident that a mother equipped with love and understanding for her child could do as good a job as any other teacher. After seventeen years, I am even more confident of this fact—not only for myself, but for every home schooling mother.

Nevertheless, I did essentially have to learn how to teach all over again. As experience gradually taught me how to use a teacher's manual, plan a lesson, and teach phonics, my most helpful asset was my maternal knowledge of my children. Many things that teachers must learn—to love, understand, and spend time with their students—come naturally to mothers.

Therefore, as you approach the tasks of planning your schedule and choosing a curriculum, I would like to remind you from the outset that God has naturally equipped you for this job. Of course, you will want to put a great deal of thought into the choices you make for your family. But remember that you have no need to be intimidated by the methods employed by "traditional" schools. Indeed, your ability to tailor your schedule, curriculum, and teaching methods to the individual needs of your child is one that would make the best public school teachers envious!

With this in mind, then, let us look at some of the most challenging aspects of home schooling a large family: planning a schedule, choosing a curriculum, and teaching multiple age levels.

THE DAILY SCHEDULE

My addressing the subject of schedules is like Simon Peter giving a lecture on self-restraint! I have always been a schedule-hater. I would much rather have a day marked by flexibility and spontaneity than one that is planned out to every last minute—maybe because I could never follow such a plan anyway.

However, with six school-age children and a toddler to manage in the process, it has become necessary for me to maintain some semblance of a daily schedule—whether it be a loose one or a rigid one. In fact, as our family has changed throughout the years, so has our daily routine.

When I began home schooling, I had three girls: Christy, Jayme, and Katie. Because my children were young and the school day was relatively short, I was able to keep a fairly flexible daily routine.

Mornings were dedicated to activities involving all three of my daughters. The very first activity of our school day was what we called "Special Time," a short devotion time in which we sang, memorized Scripture, read a Bible story, and prayed. Although throughout the years our schedule has drastically changed along with our growing family, we have continued doing "Special Time" every school day.

On many occasions, I have been tempted to set aside this devotion time and get on with the academic portion of the day, especially when we were running behind schedule. However, whenever that temptation came, I would always remember that the very purpose for our home schooling was to teach our children God's truth "as we walk along the way, when we lie down, and when we rise up" (see Deuteronomy 6:7). Our "Special Time" has been the one structured way that we obey this command on a daily basis, and I feel it is very important to maintain it as a fixed part of the schedule.

Even though it sometimes makes us late, I have given "Special Time" precedence over our academic instruction. As a result, I believe that God has greatly blessed us, both by giving us good spiritual results and by giving us good academic results with our children. God's promise in Matthew 6:33 has certainly proven true: "But seek first His kingdom, and His righteousness; *and all these things shall be added to you* (emphasis added).

After "Special Time," we used to spend about an hour cleaning one section of the house. I had divided the house into five sections, and every school day we would clean one section   scrubbing the toilets, mopping the kitchen floor, or vacuuming the carpets. If time remained before lunch, we would spend it in a fun activity—going to the library, baking, or doing an art project.

After lunch, two-year-old Katie took an afternoon nap. While she slept, I would spend about two hours of intensive instruction time with Christy. First, we would discuss her schoolwork from the previous day, which I had corrected in the evening. Then we would go over that day's new assignments, which I had planned the previous weekend, and written in a weekly assignment book.

While Christy and I worked, five-year-old Jayme would either entertain herself or eavesdrop on Christy's lessons. In fact, she became so interested in what Christy was learning that she essentially taught herself to read that year. I soon had an active little kindergartner studying alongside my second-grader.

After Christy finished her schoolwork and Katie woke up from her nap, it was time to begin preparing dinner. My daughters would either help me in the kitchen or spend time playing on their own.

In the evenings, I set aside time to correct Christy's work and go over the next day's assignments. Although it initially took only about an hour to correct and review assignments each evening, the time increased as my family got larger.

I maintained this rather flexible routine for five years, as we added Jessica and Angela to our family. Around this time, Mike also became involved in our schooling, taking on the responsibility of teaching math, science, and history to the older girls for a few years. This helped ease my load and was also a good chance for Mike to play a more active role in the education of his children.

Finally, however, after the birth of our sixth child, Michael, I began to realize the need for a more fixed schedule. Despite my dislike for schedules in general, the pressure of teaching and mothering a family of six was getting to be too much without an organized daily plan. So in August 1988, Mike and I sat down to draw up an hour-by-hour daily schedule for the coming school year. We have continued to keep this general format since then, adjusting it as necessary each year.

One of the primary changes about our new schedule was that we eliminated the evening and weekend time I spent correcting and planning assignments. Instead, as I spent time working with each child individually, I corrected work and gave assignments on the spot. When a child was not meeting with me, she was either helping with the younger children or working on "homework."

Another change we made was to catch Jayme up to Christy and work with the two of them together for most subjects. They were the only two children we have done this with so far, but it did work beautifully with them. Jayme was ready for more challenging work, and Christy seemed to enjoy working along with Jayme. They were "classmates" throughout their high school years.

Thus, for several years, our schedule looked something like this:

9:00 - 10:15	Special Time
10:15 - 11:45	Work with Katie
	(Christy and Jayme watch little ones)
11:45 - 12:45	Lunch and clean-up
12:45 - 3:00	Work with Christy and Jayme
	(little ones take naps)
3:00 - 4:00	Mom's walk!

However, as the number of grade levels in our family's home school began to increase, another adjustment became necessary. With our schedule as it was, some of my children had to wait until the end of the day to meet with me and receive their assignments. This meant they were often busy working on schoolwork until bedtime.

Just a few years ago, we came up with a new plan. I now meet with each child twice a day, going over half of the subjects in the morning and half in the afternoon. The children now have "morning work" and "afternoon work" that they must complete before their meetings with me. Each child has an assignment book to help him or her stay on track. I am still able to correct assignments on the spot, but every child now has work to be done throughout the day.

This new approach is reflected in our 1998-1999 schedule. It looks a bit more complicated than the first schedule, but it worked pretty well!

1998-1999

School Year Schedule

9:00 - 9:05	Opening exercises (flag salute, Bible reading, prayer)
9:05 - 9:45	Emily
9:45 - 10:25	Michael
10:25 - 11:15	Angie
11:15 - 12:15	Jessica
12:15 - 12:45	Lunch for everyone
12:45 - 1:15	Kids clean up (except Emily)
12:45 - 1:25	Emily
1:25 - 2:15	Special Time
2:15 - 2:55	Michael
2:55 - 3:50	Jessica
3:50 - 4:35	Angie

Johnny & Joey's schedule (taught by Jayme)

9:05 - 10:15	Joey
10:15 - 12:00	Johnny

Peter-watching duty

9:05 - 9:45	Michael
9:45 - 10:25	Emily
10:25 - 11:15	Jessica
11:15 - 12:15	Angie
12:15 - 1:15	Peter eats lunch with everyone else
1:15 - 4:00	Peter's naptime

I will be the first to admit that there has never been a day when we were able to stick exactly to our schedule. It's impossible to anticipate the unexpected late nights, illnesses, phone calls, and special projects that can throw off the best-laid plans. However, our schedule does provide the general framework for our school day. When tempered with an attitude of flexibility, it is the way that works best for our family.

If you are searching for a way to schedule your own home school day, remember that there are almost as many different methods as there are home schooling families. One family I know completes all their instruction in the morning before the little ones get up. The mother and older children wake up at 5:00, begin school at 6:00, and are finished by 8:30 or 9:00. If you are an early riser, this may be the solution for you.

I know of other families who instruct all of their children in one room at one time, with the mother going from child to child to correct work or explain concepts as needed. Although this approach generally works best for families with slightly fewer school-age children, it can be a very effective way to get instruction done in a shorter amount of time.

While some families prefer writing out daily assignments for their children like we do now, others write out weekly (or even monthly) assignment sheets. Curricula like Calvert or Sonlight have master teacher's planners containing the assignments for the entire school year, and many families have found these to be very helpful for planning out weeks at a time.

In terms of a year-round schedule, our family has always taken a summer break that roughly coincides with the public school calendar. I know of several families who choose to work year-round, giving them the freedom to take time off throughout the year. A good friend of mine teaches her children through the summer months, but she takes off the entire month of December. Others work only four days a week but continue their studies throughout the entire calendar year. For me, summer is a much-needed break, and I am usually as ready for it as the kids are!

Again, I would stress that I have never been able to completely adhere to my schedule, even on the best of days. It helps me to remember that my schedule is a guide, not a dictator. I have also found it necessary at times to make changes in my schedule midway through the year, adjusting things that have become burdensome or difficult. As my family and our circumstances have changed, so has our daily plan. Flexibility has helped me stay sane!

What about Curriculum?

The curriculum we choose affects almost every aspect of our school day. No wonder it is such a hot topic among home school moms!

A few weeks ago, my friend Geni Hall talked me into "guest-hosting" a chat session for her online home school support group. Since I am computer-illiterate, my daughter Jayme sat at the keyboard, typing out my responses to the questions asked by other home schooling mothers. Despite the unfamiliar medium, I found the topics of conversation to be very familiar. I was not surprised when, about two minutes into the chat session, someone asked: "What curriculum do you use?" In the discussion that followed, it became obvious that no two home school programs represented that night were exactly alike. Some mothers preferred the traditional textbook approach, others liked unit studies, and still others designed their own curriculum. I saw a wide range of abilities, creativity, family styles, and time commitments, just as I do at home school conferences.

I have always used traditional textbooks with my children. Although we do pick and choose from different curriculum suppliers, we primarily use A Beka, BJU Press, and Saxon Math. The subjects we cover are fairly basic: math, grammar, reading, spelling, penmanship, history, and science. (Although when we first started home schooling, I rarely taught history and science—I had my hands full just learning how to teach the three Rs!)

As I work with each child on a daily basis, I give him or her an assignment from each textbook. In every subject area, we work our way through the entire textbook during our nine-month school year (although we have been known to fall short of "finishing the book" in a few instances!).

I know many mothers who like to use unit studies and other creative options with their children, but I am simply more comfortable with the traditional approach for my family. I have never been particularly creative myself, choosing instead to concentrate on the basics. Textbooks help me to feel sure that we are covering everything. I also feel that a unity-study approach would be too time-consuming for my large family and that it would be difficult for me to handle with a wide range of age groups.

For mothers like me, I would encourage you that it's okay not to be ultra-creative with your curriculum. My goal has always been simply to give my children the tools of general knowledge and good study skills, and that has certainly not deterred them from being creative on their own. I am constantly finding them elbow-deep in extracurricular projects, experiments, and crafts. From science experiments to water-color paintings to Civil War reenactments, they have demonstrated a love for learning that extends beyond the "classroom." At the same time, because of my focus on the basics, I can be confident that they have some solid academic training under their belts.

However, I certainly do not want to discourage those mothers who have the creativity, energy, and time to use a more unique approach with their children. As I have said before, every family is different. A unit-study curriculum, such as Konos, may be just what you need to motivate and excite you and your children. It also provides a wonderful way for your entire family to learn together. Of course, a family may choose to do a unit study in a few specific subjects (like science or history), while using more traditional textbooks for other subjects.

There are many other curriculum options as well. One very large family in our church has used the A Beka home school videos for certain subjects, especially for their high school age children. Video-schooling has helped this family stay afloat in a sea of grade levels. Our older girls also used the A Beka videos for learning French in high school. Although they did enjoy learning a foreign language that way, they found that the traditional classroom structure tended to be rather time-consuming. Taking a video "French class" gave Jayme and Katie their first taste of what it is like to wait for other students.

I know of other families who use correspondence courses to ease the mother's burden of correcting work and giving assignments. Other curricula, such as School of Tomorrow (ACE) and Alpha Omega, provide learning booklets which allow the children to study on their own and correct their own work. Either of these options can be used for all your children or for only a few of them.

A curriculum like Calvert or Sonlight provides mothers with a lot of guidance and structure. Master teacher's planners for each grade contain assignments for the entire year. I know of several families in our church who use this option with great success.

Home school support groups will often provide teaching co-ops for certain subjects. In our area, several families have gotten together for art and science lessons once a week. This can be a great way both to supplement academic areas in which you are less confident and to fellowship with other home schooling families.

Almost every home schooling mother will look at the available options differently. The very methods that invigorate and excite some women will make others feel tired just thinking about them. I have never found it helpful to force myself into a mold that simply does not fit me. Do not be afraid to experiment as you try to find the approach that works best for you and your family.

Toddlers to Teenagers— the Challenge of Multiple Age Levels

Who says the life of a home schooling mother does not present diverse challenges? In the space of one day, I must struggle to balance high school algebra and fifth grade science with third grade reading and dirty diapers. In fact, teaching multiple age levels while caring for little ones is probably the biggest challenge for any home schooling mother.

The question of what to do with our toddlers and babies during the school hours is a struggle for many home schooling mothers, this mom included. There is no easy answer to this question, and no solution ever works 100 percent of the time. I think above all else we need to trust God on a daily basis to give us wisdom and great patience with our little ones as we try to faithfully teach our older children. Our God is a big God, and He will provide what will work for you.

I can, however, share with you some things we have tried over the years to "solve" this problem, along with some ideas I have heard from other moms. For several years we had our older children watch the young ones on a rotational basis. Although we are currently functioning this way once again, with the older children caring for the little ones, there were several years when this arrangement was not feasible. After Christy and Jayme graduated from high school, they both began working full time. Our house was unusually full of little ones at the time, and they proved too much for our older school age children to handle. After considering the problem, Mike and I decided to hire a nanny, or "mother's helper," to come over on weekday mornings.

Our mother's helpers proved to be an answer to prayer. Our children still talk fondly of Dana, a young woman who helped us during the 1993-1994 school year. She would usually be at our house three or four days a week, for five to six hours a day. Dana's jobs included watching the little ones, straightening the house, and folding laundry. After Dana left Virginia to pursue missions, we had two more successive nannies over a period of two years. Although we no longer need a mother's helper in our home, this was a real solution for us in a time of need.

Of course, a nanny is not always affordable or feasible. Some mothers take care of little ones during school hours by keeping a special toy box, or play area, that is designated only for school hours. For a toddler, this can turn a time of separation from Mom into a special treat. Other mothers may opt to keep their younger children with them during instruction time, especially babies and infants. Also, husbands with more flexible work hours may be able to help out with the little ones during school time. In moments of desperation we have also resorted to using a short Christian video to entertain our preschoolers.

But it is not only the little ones who present a challenge. Some mothers fear the high school years more than the "terrible twos." When a child reaches high school, a whole host of new questions arise. What about advanced classes? Can my child still play sports? How can I teach a foreign language? Fortunately, in today's world, the options for home schooled high schoolers abound. My daughter Katie spent much of her junior and senior years of high school traveling to our local community college for courses in French, business, and calculus. Katie was also active throughout her high school years at the local Christian school, participating in their athletics program. In fact, the Christian school in our area allows home schoolers to participate in any classes they choose, from track to chemistry to algebra.

Correspondence schools and tutors provide other options for high school level courses. We had our first experience with tutoring the year that Mike ran for lieutenant governor of Virginia. When he first considered launching his campaign in the fall of 1992, we had eight children. Three of our children were under age six, and five were of school age. Christy and Jayme were in their senior year of high school. With such a diverse group of grade levels, and with Mike considering a run for statewide office, the school year certainly presented its challenges. One of the biggest was: "What will we do about teaching Christy and Jayme?" For many years, Mike had been teaching them science, math, and history, and I did not think I could handle the extra task of teaching those subjects at high school level.

One day, shortly before the beginning of the school year, we received an unexpected answer to prayer. One of the lawyers at HSLDA (who was himself a home schooling father of six) offered to tutor Christy and Jayme in geometry and biology twice a week for the entire school year. The girls were somewhat unsure of this arrangement at first, but they were quickly won over after their first lesson with Scott Somerville. A Harvard graduate, he seemed born to teach. The girls learned a great deal that year and count it as one of the highlights of their high school years. In this case, a knowledgeable home school parent proved to be the solution for a tutor. With video and Internet classes becoming more widespread, the opportunities for tutoring in difficult subjects are multiplying.

One positive aspect of the high school years is that a mother's teaching load can actually lighten as her children become more responsible. When my oldest daughters reached high school, I only had to meet with them once or twice a week to go over assignments and corrections. Christy and Jayme essentially taught themselves Algebra 2 during their junior year, working through their Saxon textbook, correcting their own homework, and consulting me whenever they couldn't understand a concept. Katie's community college courses eliminated almost all my teaching burden during her senior year.

Another positive element of multiple age levels is the potential for your older children to help with the younger ones. This can even extend beyond childcare and into teaching responsibilities. In Christy and Jayme's senior year of high school, they taught a biology "class" for their younger siblings. They simplified the material they were learning in their own biology curriculum and taught it to the little ones during my instructional time with Katie. This proved to be beneficial both for the little ones, who had fun learning all about mammals, but also for the older girls, who found that teaching is truly the best way to learn. My older children have also taught their younger siblings in less structured ways. On many occasions, the younger children have learned the alphabet, how to count, or how to write simple words from an older brother or sister.

When my son Jonathan reached kindergarten age in the fall of 1997, I had no idea how I was going to find time to teach him. My day was already full instructing the oldest four school-age children. What's more, I knew that four-year-old Joseph would be ready to start school the following year.

At the time, Jayme was doing missions work in Romania. With the end of the year approaching, she was in the process of deciding whether or not to stay an additional year, as she had been invited to do. One day during her weekly phone call home, she told me she felt that God wanted her to come back home to help me. I had been hoping and praying that Jayme might consider that very possibility, but I truly wanted her to determine for herself what God wanted her to do! "Thank You so much, Lord!" I prayed silently as Jayme told me of her decision. She returned in December and started doing kindergarten work with Johnny in January. This past year, she taught both Johnny and Joey in all subjects.

It is impossible to predict the challenging circumstances that can arise within a family from year to year. Illnesses, new births, special events, moves, and financial circumstances can all drastically impact a home school program. As I mentioned earlier, there were several years when I honestly did not know how I was going to make it through our nine months of school. Nevertheless, I have always seen God's provision in these special cases, sometimes just in the nick of time. When I simply trusted and obeyed, He caused the details to fall into place.

In Everything Give Thanks

Whenever I speak publicly about the practicalities of home schooling a large family, I start off with two basic reminders for the mothers in the audience.

The first is best illustrated by a letter I clipped from *The Teaching Home* several years ago. Written by a home schooling mother from North Carolina, it reads:

> One morning I was trying to help seven-year-old Ryan with his math, and our toddler, Earl, was repeatedly bothering him despite my efforts to keep him entertained. He started to pull on Ryan's pencil and would not let go.

I let out a sigh and started looking out the window daydreaming about how it would be if I just had two or three children and no little ones around. I never said anything to anyone out loud, but I though of all the hours of uninterrupted schoolwork that we could get done, the great unit studies and crafts that we could do, and the great wealth of knowledge that my children could have.

"Mommy," Ryan called out, and his voice brought me back to reality. "I'd rather be dumb and have Earlie than be very smart and not have him." His words hit me like a ton of bricks.

It occurred to me to make sure I kept my priorities the way they should be.

Toddlers and babies take naps, and we can schedule subjects that demand complete attention for those times.

We may not take all the field trips that we'd like, due to the sheer hassle of getting six young children ready, but it causes us to spend more relaxed time at home instead of rushing about.

We spend more time reading out loud when there is a newborn who needs lots of nursing and cuddling.

True, we may get fewer "projects" done, but my children are developing into real servants who like to help their siblings. Aren't our children our ultimate "projects" anyway? The joy that the little ones bring to us far surpasses any craft or science project or field trip.

As for Ryan, he got his pencil back and finished his math. He has tested very well and gone on far above "grade level" in most subjects.

As I thought about his words that day, I realized that I have a very wise little boy who has a lot to teach his mother.

This mother learned a lesson that none of us should forget: our young children are a tremendous blessing for the entire family. The "challenge of multiple age levels" is a good problem to have! I have spoken with so many women who would love to have more children, but are unable to. Others, who have watched their youngest child leave home, would love to have some of those years back again. Be thankful for the time you have with your little ones. The time for getting "important projects" done will come all too soon. The time with your "ultimate projects"—your children—is shorter than you think.

The second reminder is one that I have already emphasized: it is impossible to do this job without God's strength. Remember this truth even as you go about the practical business of choosing your curriculum and planning out your schedule. Curriculum and schedules are helpful tools, but they are not "miracle solutions" that will make us perfect teachers and mothers. Our hope is in God alone.

"The horse is made ready for the day of battle, but the victory belongs to the LORD" (Proverbs 21:31, RSV).

Where no oxen are, the manger is clean, but much increase comes by the strength of the ox.

PROVERBS 14:4

6

SOAP SUDS,
SHOPPING TRIPS, AND
SOCCER PRACTICE

Running This Crazy Home

O kay Mom, so I'm supposed to take Michael to Lincoln Elementary, and Jessica to Franklin Park?"

"Yes, and don't forget to go by the Matzkers' and pick up Holly on the way to Franklin. They said they could give Jessica a ride home. And you'll have time to go by the grocery store to pick up those noodles for dinner on your way back, right?"

"Yep. But I won't be back in time to pick up Emily. Are you doing that?"

"Actually, Dad said he could get her on the way to Angie's practice. I need to stay here, because Peter's still napping. I'm just going to work on this laundry until you get home, and then I was hoping to go for a walk."

"Okay, great. Call me on my cell phone if you think of anything else you need at the store."

The above conversation is no exaggeration. In fact, it is quite typical for a weekday in our home, especially during softball and soccer season. Needless to say, the job of a home schooling mother does not end when the teaching is done. There is still the house to clean, dinner to cook, errands to run, laundry to do, and children to raise.

I often hear from mothers who wonder just exactly how I manage all these duties. "Don't you just go crazy with everything there is to do?" one woman asked. "I only have five children, and I can barely stay on top of everything."

Honestly, there have been many days when I did feel that I was going crazy. The tasks can seem endless, and the pace dizzying. On some days I cannot remember having sat down for two minutes. Those are the "stormy" days—days on which I especially need God's supernatural strength.

However, while almost no day in our home could be described as "slow-paced," our lives usually manage to fall somewhere between "moderate" and "stressed frenzy." Despite my occasional bouts with the craziness of our household, my long-term sanity has remained relatively intact.

In this chapter, I would like to share with you some of the ways that I have managed to keep my home running over the years and still stay sane. Again, I feel the need to stress that each family is unique, and these methods are simply the ones that have worked best for us. Look at this as one woman's personal story and pick out anything that may be useful to you.

KEEPING THINGS CLEAN

I don't know about you, but a messy house depresses me. As I shared earlier, I grew up in an immaculate household—my mother still organizes her spice rack alphabetically! Although I will never be as organized as she is, it does seem that I can think, live, and feel better in orderly surroundings.

However, having ten children has certainly taught me to relax a bit. For many years, I tried to keep the house continually straightened up during the school day. While I was able to do this when our household was smaller, it began to get increasingly difficult every year. Finally, we reached the point where my attempts to constantly keep the house in order were taking up too much of our school time. As Mike and I sat down to write out our daily schedule that year, he said, "Vickie, I just want to set a few specific times for cleaning up the house. During the rest of the time, I think you should just let things go a bit."

It was not easy for me to do at first. But now we simply have a few times during the day when we all work together to straighten up the house: after lunch, after the end of school, and after dinner. Of course, there is always a little "maintenance" that goes on, and I am still working on training my children to clean up after themselves more consistently. But I have found a bit of freedom in setting aside a few specific time slots for straightening the house, and "letting things go" between times.

While I do have ultimate responsibility for the care of our home, I am certainly a believer in spreading out the work among all the members of the household. My children are all expected to help keep the house in regular order. The younger children are usually assigned to clean up their own rooms, as well as the basement play area. The older children have more responsibility, helping to clean up the main areas of the house as well as their own rooms.

I know many families who have an organized system of dividing up the chores among their children. For instance, on a certain day one child will be assigned to wash the dishes, another child sweeps the floor, and another takes out the garbage. For many families, this system is a great way to ensure that everything gets done and that everyone does his or her part. When we tried this method, however, we found that it was difficult to cover every situation that might arise. In a house where people were often gone for piano lessons, soccer practice, or ballet, some chores fell through the cracks.

In our family, there are only a few chores that we assign to specific people. Michael, Emily, Jonathan, and Joseph are on a rotating schedule to feed our dog. Emily and Michael are expected to clear the breakfast dishes and put them in the sink. Jessica and Angie have the regular task of folding laundry. But for most regular day-to-day housekeeping, we maintain this simple system:

Everyone who is available pitches in until the job is done. This way, everyone does a part, but we are also able to retain some flexibility for special situations.

Besides the day-to-day work of keeping the house in order, every mother also deals with the more intensive job of cleaning house: vacuuming carpets, cleaning bathrooms, mopping floors, and cleaning windows. There have been several ways that we have handled these duties over the years.

I found a creative way to keep my house clean during the first several years of home schooling. I divided the house up into five sections, and my daughters and I would clean one section each school day. Because our schooling only required a few hours in the afternoon at that time, mornings were free for cleaning and other projects.

Some time after the birth of our fifth child, our daily schedule became too busy for this method of house-cleaning. At that time, I found that by simply assigning a little extra schoolwork on each day, I could rearrange our schedule into a four-day school week. Monday through Thursday, we studied as usual. Fridays became either cleaning day or errand day—we alternated every other week. Everyone was expected to pitch in on cleaning day, either helping to clean the house or taking a turn watching the youngest children. For several years, this method both kept our home clean and taught my daughters how to keep house.

When I was pregnant with our seventh child, I began to feel the pinch of squeezing five schooldays into four. With Christy and Jayme about to enter high school, I knew that their schoolwork would require more and more time from them. For my part, I was feeling the stress of handling my growing family.

As Mike and I talked over the daily schedule that year, I was fretting about how busy we were going to be. "Vickie," he said, "I really think we should consider getting a cleaning lady to come in and clean house for us. We can afford it, and it would give you time for more important things."

I had heard Mike make this suggestion before, and I had always resisted the idea. Of course I can clean my own house! I always thought, somewhat indignantly. Of all the home schooling mothers I knew, only a very few of them had cleaning ladies. It seemed too easy, somehow, or perhaps even a mark of incompetence on my part. How could I look my fellow home schooling moms in the eye and tell them that I was hiring someone to clean my house for me? Then I took a step back and realized the pride behind this way of thinking. If this is my best argument against getting a cleaning lady, I thought, then it's not a very good one. I realized that with a cleaning lady, I would have a little more time to devote to being a good teacher and mother. As Mike said, those were "more important things." My children were a higher priority than proving my own housekeeping ability.

We have had a cleaning lady for the past eight years. For the first few years she came every other week, and then we switched to weekly cleanings. Our current cleaning lady takes only a few hours to clean our house, and she is able to work around us as we continue with our regular school day. Considering the way our schedule has become, with more children in school than ever, this extra help is a tremendous blessing for us.

"Spring cleaning" at our house actually takes place in the summer time. As soon as school is out, I launch into my summer organization projects: cleaning out the garage, organizing drawers and shelves throughout the house, and going through each of the children's clothing. My children have their own jobs of clearing out clutter in their desks, on their shelves, and in all their little personal nooks and crannies. After a long winter of books and studies, I actually enjoy the chance to turn the house upside down and make it a little more livable.

"Mom's Jobs"—Laundry and Cooking

Although our housekeeping chores have always been fairly evenly split among all family members, there are a few jobs that remain primarily mine. Our family's laundry is my constant companion. Although my oldest daughters started doing their own laundry several years ago, I still wash clothes for most of the household. My electric washing machine and clothes dryer are invaluable tools (my hat is off to women who dry their clothes on clotheslines—I do not know how they do it).

On average, our family probably puts out about six to eight loads of laundry a week. I sometimes try to keep up with the laundry during weekdays, taking a few minutes here and there to put in a load or two. However, weekends are usually my best time to get caught up on all the washing and drying.

Jessica and Angie do have the job of folding all the laundry and putting it away. They like to sit in our family room and listen to tapes of "Adventures in Odyssey"—a Christian kids' radio program—while surrounded by the mounds of clothing. They and the other girls also help me with the mending and ironing, of which I do very little.

The other job that has always been my primary responsibility is the cooking for our family. While cooking has certainly never been my particular joy, I do enjoy providing my family with a big home-cooked dinner. In fact, dinner is the one big meal that we eat all together as a family.

Breakfast is a very casual meal in our family, with cold cereal as the main attraction. (Guests at our home invariably comment on the ten to twenty cereal boxes that grace the top of our refrigerator.) Although my oldest daughters grew up on Cheerios, Shredded Wheat, and my good intentions, Mike's sweet tooth has prevailed in later years. Our cereal selection now features plenty of Froot Loops and Lucky Charms.

Lunches are also usually casual, and most of the children make lunch for themselves. We encourage leftovers for lunch (this suggestion, however, is not always followed). During this past school year, one of my older girls would usually get lunch for the youngest boys— often a sandwich or a "snack plate," a sampling of lunch meat, fruit, cheese or yogurt, and crackers.

Around 6:00 in the evening, I begin dinner preparations, which usually take about an hour. I know many families who like to set aside one or two days a month to make all their dinners for that month, creating a supply of frozen meals ready to warm up each evening. For those who might like to try this method, home school book fairs and catalogues usually sell books that explain the details and suggest appropriate recipes. I, however, have just never felt motivated to do this—the prospect of one or two full days of cooking is less appealing to me than one hour each evening! I have always stuck to the traditional approach of preparing one meal each night for the family.

Our main dishes are usually fairly simple and feature meat (which is certainly to Mike's taste). While I try to avoid excessive fat and sugar, and provide a balance of protein, starch, vegetables, and fruits, I would not describe myself as a "health nut" in the meals I cook for my family. In fact, in watching my own calorie intake, I often avoid certain dishes that I have cooked for the rest of the family, loading up instead on those foods that work better with my metabolism.

Once in a while, my older girls will give me a break and do the cooking. To my delight, each of my daughters enjoys cooking and baking more than I do. In recent years, Christy, Jayme, and Katie have taken over our holiday meal preparations. For several months last year, Jayme cooked dinner every night, before her own schedule became too busy. When Christy and Katie lived at home, they also helped with dinners whenever they could. Jessica and Angie are also starting to help me out by making more simple dinners on particularly hectic days.

This summer, Mike has even been pitching in to help with dinners, in order to free me up for my summer organization projects. While his cooking abilities are limited, he greatly helps out by barbecuing on the outdoor grill, or bringing home something for dinner—fried chicken, pizza, or the ingredients for sub sandwiches.

Although it certainly requires time and work on my part, cooking a family dinner is certainly worth the effort for me. With the busy schedules of the older family members, dinnertime is often the only time the entire family can be together during the day. It is also often the time when Christy and Katie will come over with their husbands. Dinner is certainly one of the highlights of the day, no matter if the menu is pot roast or pancakes.

GOING OUT—ERRANDS AND ACTIVITIES

There is a standing joke in our family that if the actual Vickie Farris ever went to our supermarket to buy groceries, the store employees would faint. My husband and daughters have been going on my behalf for so many years that they have now become well known for the large amount of groceries that they always purchase.

It was not always this way. For many years, I ran the family's errands and did all the grocery shopping myself. When I had only three or four children, my schedule allowed me the time to go out with my daughters in the morning. When we later switched to a four-day school schedule, on Friday errand days, I would pile all the children in the van, and we would go out together—to the library, supermarket, and other stores.

Today, things are somewhat different. My schedule no longer has a regular time for running errands. Instead, Mike and Jayme cover most grocery shopping and errand duties. Because Jayme's busy schedule sends her into town on a daily basis, it is usually easy for her to go places to do favors for me. Mike is also very faithful to call whenever he is on his way home, asking if there is anything I need from town. I usually make a big shopping list once a week, and on weekends one of them will do the job of buying all the family groceries.

Our children's extracurricular activities are another cause for our family's seemingly constant motion. Jessica, Angie, Michael, Emily, and Jonathan are all currently active participants in both spring and fall sports. Athletics have always been important in our family and the local sports and recreation leagues are also a good chance to interact with our neighbors. In addition, Mike has been a girls' softball coach for years—Christy, Jayme, Katie, and Angie have all called him "coach" at one point in their childhood. Sports have been a great way for Mike to interact with his children.

In addition to sports, we also have had our share of music lessons. Almost all of our children have taken piano lessons; Christy and Jessica have been our two enthusiasts so far. In fact, Christy is now our piano teacher for Jessica, Michael, and Emily. An added benefit of this arrangement is that she can come to our house to give the lessons.

Another all-consuming activity at one point was dance—Jayme took ballet and tap-dancing lessons for ten years. Because her dance studio was a twenty-minute drive from our house, her lessons consumed the most driving time. Before she was able to drive herself, Mike, Christy, and I took turns with the driving duty.

I am delighted to see my children actively participating in activities outside the home. However, I cannot deny that it is sometimes a strain on the schedule, especially in the height of soccer or softball season. Our afternoons, evenings, and Saturdays are practically consumed by practices and games. The constant driving to and from sports events falls mostly on Jayme and me, with Mike helping whenever he can. When the children asked about playing basketball in the winter, I put my foot down and said no. The winter and summer months are our times to recover from soccer in the fall and softball in the spring!

Nonetheless, I enjoy the family togetherness brought about by our participation in sports. The whole family, including sons-in-law, often ends up on the sidelines or in the bleachers, cheering together for one of the children. After the game, we often go out to eat or have a casual dinner together at home. It is times like these, along with the satisfaction I see on the faces of our little athletes, that make all the driving time worthwhile.

WHO DOES THE "MAN'S WORK?"

My oldest girls used to laughingly identify with a certain passage in Nehemiah, which listed all the Hebrew families who repaired sections of the wall in Jerusalem. There was one verse in particular that caught their attention: "...Shallum the son of Hallohesh, the official of half the district of Jerusalem, made repairs, he and his daughters" (Nehemiah 3:12).

Mike has often joked that he was born without a handyman gene. He never has been one to repair or build things around the house, although he did put in many years of faithful service mowing the lawn. We have roughly two acres of lawn, and another acre of what we call "the field." The work of raking and bagging the cut grass fell to Christy, Jayme, and Katie. They also took responsibility for trimming the bushes and the occasional weeding between the flagstones.

When Mike ran for lieutenant governor in 1993, Katie took over the job of mowing the lawn until her allergies forced her to stop. With the boys still too young for this task, we decided just a few years ago to hire a lawn service. As soon as Michael gets old enough to do the job, we intend to hand the reins to him.

The men in our church have often surprised us by helping us out during times when Mike was unusually busy or out of town. On several occasions during the campaign, we had one home schooling father after another coming out to handle a flood in the basement or look at a leaky faucet. Just recently, another friend from church helped us solve a plumbing emergency which threatened to leave us without water for three days.

Our sons-in-law have been another surprising source of handy work around the house and yard. Just a month ago, Christy's husband, Rich, spent the better part of a Saturday clearing out a particularly overgrown corner of our yard, enlisting the help of Michael, Johnny, and Joey. We have greatly enjoyed having two more adult males around the house for hammering, hoisting, and hauling duties.

WE'RE ALL IN THIS TOGETHER

I cannot deny that running a household of twelve people is a special challenge. There are certainly occasions when I have to pick up after my husband and older children, and it is always a challenge to keep track of everyone's schedules. However, despite the fact that having ten children certainly is a lot of work, I also have quite a bit of help from my older children. As you imagine what it would be like to run a large family, do not forget that, by the time your younger children are born, your older children will actually be adults-in-training.

Mike and I had five daughters before we had our first son. I remember praying and praying for sons, wondering why God just kept giving us girls. Today, I am extremely thankful that He chose to give us our girls first. My daughters have been an incredible help to me over the years, and I do not know how I would have handled things without them.

What is more, our joint work to run this crazy household has given me an immeasurably closer relationship with my daughters than I would have otherwise had. I cannot tell you how many times we have been together in the kitchen at the end of the day, wearily laughing over the day's chaos. For me, who never had sisters, this is a special blessing. Working together always brings about a unique closeness in any relationship.

Likewise, I believe that working together to raise our children and run our home has strengthened my marriage with Mike. Undoubtedly, there have been times when excessive work threatened to come between us, and our large family has certainly lessened the time we are able to spend alone together. However, as long as I keep Mike in his proper place as my priority, second only to God, our joint work, focus, and vision is actually a great strength. (I will share more about these marital issues in a later chapter.)

Just as it is vital for me to remember that my work at home is work done in obedience to God, so my children need to have that same biblical foundation for the work they do around the house. For them, the foundation can be as simple as: "Children, obey your parents in the Lord, for this is right" (Ephesians 6:1). But as soon as they are old enough to understand, Mike and I make it a point to tell them exactly why this lifestyle is God's command for our family.

It is exciting to see your children become your coworkers in the Lord's work. As you work to raise your children and run your household, remember that you're all in it together.

"Whatever you do, do your work heartily, as for the Lord rather than for men" (Colossians 3:23).

With all my heart I have sought Thee; do not let me wander from Thy commandments.

PSALM 119:10

7

MARY
VS.
MARTHA

Putting the Lord and His Priorities First

By Monday, I already knew it was going to be one of those weeks. We woke up that morning tired after a busy weekend, and the school day got started later than usual. The laundry was piled up in the hamper, and the house was generally in disorder. Halfway through the day, I remembered that we were scheduled to take dinner that night to a family in our church, who had just had a new baby. Unfortunately, we also had a softball game at 6:00, rescheduled after Saturday's rain.

Tuesday looked no better. We had to rush through our school day, because I had agreed to watch the children of a friend that afternoon. My oldest daughter, pregnant and feeling very sick, called to ask if someone could come over to do a little cleaning at her house. More softball practices required our attention that evening, and Mike had a meeting to attend until late at night.

Wednesday and Thursday found me growing more tired and grouchy by the minute. On several occasions, I was just about to start correcting schoolwork when I got a phone call from a friend who urgently needed a listening ear. On top of all that, I was struggling to complete an article for the church newsletter by Thursday's deadline. The youngest children seemed to require even more attention than usual, we were hopelessly off our school schedule, the house was simply refusing to get clean, and Mike and the older girls were not helping like I wanted them to.

By Friday, I had reached the point of explosion. It seemed I was spending my life helping others, but nobody was helping me. I finally slumped into a chair and threw my hands in the air. "I can't do all this!" I said to no one in particular. "I need help!"

It was then that I realized something: it had been several days, at least, since I had spent any quiet time with the Lord, just enjoying His presence and getting perspective and direction from Him. I immediately thought about Martha in the Bible. She was so busy and distracted with all the good things she was doing—

things to serve Jesus Himself, her guest—that she neglected what was most important: sitting at Jesus' feet. Like me, Martha got angry with her sister Mary for failing to help her, and she even doubted whether the Lord cared about her.

It is so easy for busy home schooling moms to become like Martha. When you are struggling to juggle the demands of teaching, housekeeping, being a mother, and being a wife, your personal quiet time with God is often the first thing to be set aside. "I'll do my devotions in the afternoon, while the baby is sleeping," you say, as you quickly rush around in the morning to get breakfast for the kids. But during the baby's naptime, a friend calls for some needed counsel, or several piles of dirty laundry scream at you for washing, or…the distractions are potentially endless. Before you know it, another day has gone by and you have not even opened your Bible. Believe me, I know—I've done it!

I also know, however, that when I neglect my daily time with the Lord, I begin to dry up inside. I lose my inner joy and peace, and I begin to feel the effects of burnout. I am not very pleasant to be with, either! But most importantly, my heart begins to grow cold toward the Lord, and that is dangerous. The number one priority in my life must always be my relationship with God.

When Jesus was asked to name the greatest commandment in all of Scripture, He did not mention helping the poor, making sacrifices, or doing any kind of good deeds. Rather, He quoted Deuteronomy 6:5. "And you shall love the LORD your God with all your heart and with all your soul and with all your might." Simply loving God is the greatest command for any Christian, and it should always be the most important thing in our lives.

IS MY GOAL GOD HIMSELF?

When I miscarried four pregnancies in a row, my desire to have another child began to consume my thoughts and my prayers. I simply could not face the thought that God might not give me another baby.

It was at that time that I came across a quote from Oswald Chambers in a women's Bible study book I was reading. Chambers said, "My goal is God Himself, not joy nor peace, nor even blessing, but Himself, my God." Those words really stopped me short. I had to ask myself, "Do I want God as much as I want another baby?" Or, really, "Do I want God more than I want another baby?" A whole host of additional questions came to my mind:

"Do I want His will for my life, even if it means no more babies?"

"Can I really say my goal is God Himself, not the blessings He gives me?"

"Can I say, like Habakkuk:

Though the fig tree should not blossom,
And there be no fruit on the vines,
Though the yield of the olive should fail,
And the fields produce no food,
Though the flock should be cut off from the fold,

And there be no cattle in the stalls,
Yet I will exult in the LORD,
I will rejoice in the God of my salvation"
(Habakkuk 3:17-18)?

I learned an important lesson during those painful months. If God truly has first place in my heart and life, then my desire for Him will be greater than my desire for anything else. Moreover, I will be satisfied even if He is all I have.

When we look at a human love relationship, especially a new one, it is common to see that attitude of "nothing else matters as long as we're together." Over the past few years, I have been able to see each of my oldest daughters fall in love. It is always fun to see the changes in their behavior—they suddenly have all sorts of new priorities and interests. I remember the shock waves that rippled through our family after Katie returned from a visit with Sean and his family in Texas, wearing a brand-new pair of cowboy boots! Since when was she the kind of person to wear cowboy boots? Since she fell in love with a Texan, of course.

It was also amazing to see how much time my daughters could spend talking with their beaux on the phone. It seemed that two hours every night still was not sufficient to say all that they needed to say to each other. The only thing better than talking on the phone, of course, was being together in person. I do not believe my daughters desired to spend time with their young men for the sake of the gifts, favors, or other tokens of affection they would receive. Those things were extras, really. Rather than wanting something from each other, these young couples simply wanted each other—time spent together.

Do we experience this same desire for God Himself, not just what He can do for us? Do we have the kind of longing for God that makes us willing to turn our lives upside down to be nearer to Him? Are we interested in the things of God, simply because they are associated with Him? In the midst of hardship, is our greatest desire to become closer to God, not just for Him to rescue us from difficulty?

David was in a literal desert, being hunted down by King Saul, when he penned these words: "O God, Thou art my God; I shall seek Thee earnestly; my soul thirsts for Thee, my flesh yearns for Thee, in a dry and weary land where there is no water" (Psalm 63:1).

The story of my struggle to have our tenth child had a doubly happy ending. As I began to turn my focus away from having another child and back to God, He reemerged as my desire and my delight. And it was when I delighted myself in Him that He gave me the desire of my heart—not just our tenth child, but more importantly, a closer relationship with Himself.

REALIZING GOD'S DESIRE FOR US

Centuries ago, there was a group of believers in the city of Ephesus who worked tirelessly for God. They never compromised, refusing to tolerate any wickedness. They diligently tested the teachings of anyone claiming to have a word from God. They were known for their good deeds and hard work: helping the poor, caring for the sick, taking in the alien. They even suffered persecution and hardship, and came through with their faith intact. And yet, to this Ephesian church, God gave the following message: "But I have this against you, that you have left your first love" (Revelation 2:4). Despite their hard work for God, He was about to remove them from service unless they repented and sought to restore their original relationship with Him.

Why was it that God took issue with a church that was serving Him so faithfully? The reason is simple: because God loved these believers, He wanted them to return His love more than anything else. Just as we do not want our spouses to do things for us out of a mere sense of duty, but rather because they love us, so God wants our work for Him to be motivated by love. If He were merely our Master, He would undoubtedly be content with our dutiful service. But God, in addition to being our Master, is also very much our Lover.

We need to remember that our love for God draws its life from His overwhelming love for us. His love is always the starting point, the foundation, the beginning of the story. "In this is love, not that we loved God, but that He loved us and sent His Son to be the propitiation for our sins....We love, because He first loved us" (1 John 4:10, 19).

I have to admit that it changes my perspective when I realize just how much God actually desires me to spend time with Him. It is not simply that I need that time, or that I want that time, but also that He wants it—even more than I do. And there is nothing that pleases Him more than when I put Him first in my heart and life.

From the example of Mary and Martha, we clearly see that pure love pleases God more than pure service. Because what Jesus wanted most was a love relationship, He was more pleased by Mary's faithful attention than by Martha's diligent service.

Oswald Chambers writes:

> The main thing about Christianity is not the work we do, but the relationship we maintain and the atmosphere produced by that relationship. That is all God asks us to look after, and it is the one thing that is continually assailed.

Even when assailed, however, lovers are persistent in their wooing of one another. (When Mike decided he wanted to marry me, he basically would not take no for an answer.) It amazes me to think that God is continually seeking me and wanting me to turn to Him. There have been many times when I have felt so unfaithful in my quiet times that I thought I might as well give up. "You've messed up now," Satan has tried to tell me. "You may as well not try anymore. God doesn't want to hear from people like you."

I have learned to reject this as the lie that it is. Throughout the Old Testament, God continually demonstrates His faithful love for His people, even when they are faithless. The book of Hosea in particular paints a vivid picture of this truth, portraying God as a faithful husband who wins back His adulterous wife, the nation of Israel. When we feel that we have been faithless or lacking in desire, we need to turn back to the One whose faithfulness and love are never-ending. Remember that it is His love—not ours—that is the foundation of our relationship with Him. What a comfort to know that this is a foundation that can never crumble.

FELLOWSHIP: MAKING THE RUBBER MEET THE ROAD

"Okay, Vickie," you might be thinking. "I know my relationship with God is important. I realize it should be the most important thing in my life! In fact, before I had children, I used to be able to spend a lot of time praying and reading the Bible. But with the way things are now, I just don't know how to make it work on a daily basis. I've got three children under age 5, and between them, my house, and my husband, I just don't have a free hour during the day!"

I cannot tell you how many times I have struggled with this very problem. I remember starting school one year determined to have a quiet time with God every morning before beginning my day. The first week, I managed to reach my goal—I did my devotions every morning, and I felt great! The second week, I got sick with a terrible flu that just seemed to hang on. My devotions fell by the wayside as I struggled to get better. The third week, as any mother could probably predict, all the children caught my illness. I was up late every night with sneezing, coughing, vomiting, miserable children. The fourth week, Mike and I had an extremely busy schedule that caused us to be out late every night.

And so it continued. While there is no denying that both laziness and misplaced priorities can distract us from our time with God, sometimes the circumstances are simply beyond our control. Whether such circumstances are just a part of life, or whether they are attacks from the enemy, the fact is that sometimes we simply cannot get that free hour we want.

For someone who is truly seeking a thriving relationship with the Lord, this situation can become very frustrating. Every time you think about your quiet time, you feel the guilt of a seemingly unsolvable problem. After all, how can you tell a screaming baby to wait while you finish your devotions? (And even if you could, how could you continue to pray and meditate on Scripture with all that commotion in the background?)

One day, I was talking with my friend Linda, who is the mother of eleven children, about this problem. When I expressed my frustration over not being able to get enough time with the Lord, she nodded sympathetically. "Vickie," she said, "think about that promise in Isaiah 40:11, 'He shall feed his flock like a shepherd: he shall gather the lambs with his arm, and carry them in his bosom, and shall gently lead those that are with young' (KJV). That verse has meant so much to me," Linda explained. "It's just comforting to know that he 'gently leads' those of us who have little ones. He knows our struggles. He's not going to zap us for failing to give Him a full hour every morning like we used to. But even when we can't give Him that ideal chunk of time, we can find time to meet Him in little moments throughout the day."

I have thought often about Linda's words. God does extend special grace to those of us who are caring for little ones. He will not frown on us if we use the mundane moments of life—washing dishes, running errands, or even changing diapers—as our chances to talk with Him. There are times in life when I have had to be very creative in making time to fellowship with my Lord, and I am hardly the first mother of many children to do so. Susannah Wesley was an eighteenth century Christian woman who gave birth to nineteen children (ten of whom survived, including John and Charles Wesley). I remember reading that, in the midst of her bustling household, she would occasionally lift her apron up over her face in order to have some "private" moments with the Father. If she could do it, so can we!

I started off my married life as more of a Mary than a Martha. I had the luxury of at least one free hour a day in which to pray and study God's word, and I was able to get a good quiet time on a daily basis. Even when I had one or two little ones, naptimes provided me with a free hour or two to spend with the Lord. With three, four, and five children, however, it was no longer possible to schedule my time with God during the baby's naptime. There were several years when I got up early in the morning, before my children were up, to get that time in.

As our family grew even larger, however, early mornings also became difficult. I was often up late at night cleaning the house or spending time with Mike, and there were many periods when a young baby kept my sleeping time at a minimum. During those years, I tried breaking up my time with God into two segments—a time of prayer to start off the day, and some Bible reading before I went to bed at night.

The more my undistracted devotion time was diminished, the more I sought to find little snippets of time with God throughout the day. Nowadays, I try to take every chance I can get to focus on God and talk to Him, even during some of the most down-to-earth moments. As I have already shared, my children and I read Scripture together to start the day. Just that small planting of God's Word in my mind in the morning can give me something on which to meditate during the course of the day.

One of my best times with God is my daily walk. Regardless of the weather or the length of my to-do list, I always take about an hour every day to go for a long walk—both to get some exercise and to clear my head. Although Mike has recently been walking with me as often as he can, for many years I took this walk alone with the Lord. My solitary walks are always excellent times to pray and turn my focus back on God.

Making Scripture memory a part of your daily devotion time can also help to weave God's Word throughout the rest of your day. You can recite Scripture and reflect on its meaning even when you are far from a Bible—washing dishes, sweeping the floor, or doing laundry.

If you are looking for ways to spend more time with God, what about picking up your Bible instead of a book or magazine to read while eating lunch? While I certainly think that books and magazines have their place (I am particularly partial to *World* and *Reader's Digest*), there are days when I need to use every available quiet moment as a chance to fellowship with the Lord. If you ever get time to drive in the car alone, another way to make time for God would be to turn off the radio and use that time to talk with God or meditate on His Word.

This brings me to another point: There are times when we must make the conscious choice to set something else aside in order to get the fellowship with God we need. It is in the little daily situations where our true priorities are established. A magazine beckons us when we know that our Bible needs our attention. It is a half hour before bedtime, and we can either spend the time praying or writing that thank-you note that's been put off for so long. Although there are certainly times when we can (and should) meet an urgent need or enjoy a spontaneous pleasure, there are also times when we must say no.

Jesus faced many such dilemmas during His years on earth. People who were sick and suffering—both physically and spiritually surrounded Him. He had the power to heal all of them, to give them the Living Water and the Bread of Life. And yet, despite the overwhelming need around Him, He made time for fellowship with the Father. If He could do it, we can too. The Gospels record many instances when Jesus withdrew from ministry to spend time with the Father. "But He Himself would often slip away to the wilderness and pray" (Luke 5:16).

On another occasion, "He went off to the mountain to pray, and He spent the whole night in prayer to God" (Luke 6:12).

Sometimes it is hardest to make time for God when we feel that it will be an inconvenience to others. Mark described an incident where Jesus' time with God caused a small uproar among His followers: "And in the early morning, while it was still dark, He arose and went out and departed to a lonely place, and was praying there. And Simon and his companions hunted for Him; and they found Him, and said to Him, 'Everyone is looking for You'" (Mark 1:35-37). The truth is that we cannot always do it all. There will be times when saying yes to God will involve saying no to someone else—or to ourselves.

You may want to start out with a small goal, like spending ten minutes alone with God every day. No matter what is claiming your attention—whether it is a new baby or a home school support group meeting— ten minutes of every day would belong to God. As we discussed earlier, the force of habit can be powerful in helping us remember to turn to God. Establishing a certain time of day for your regular fellowship with God is a good way to ensure that you get that time with Him daily. However, even if your schedule is unpredictable, make it a goal for yourself to spend a certain amount of time alone with God every day—whenever that time comes in. Remember that fellowship with God is a choice, and it is one that each of us desperately needs to make.

I know how difficult this sounds, because I have been in the place where I just felt like giving up and not trying to make time for fellowship. Especially when we are in the middle of a "dry spell" in our walk with God, the prospect of reciting Scripture as we do household chores may seem dauntingly over-spiritual. Of course it is not possible to continually exist on a spiritual plane and never think about the things of this life. But let me assure you that the more time you spend with God, the more your love for Him will grow. And the more your love grows, the more time you will want to spend with Him.

Just as human love can die for lack of communication and fellowship, so your love for God will wane the less you are in contact with Him. The positive aspect of this truth is that spending even a little more daily time with God will prove surprisingly refreshing, and awaken within you a thirst for more. The way to bring about a greater commitment to God is to start small. As your love and desire for Him grow, so will the time you spend in fellowship with Him.

FOCUS: KEEPING YOUR PRIORITIES INTACT

Rrrrrring! At our house, it is hard to escape the sound of a ringing phone. It is a sound that can strike fear into my heart, especially when I am feeling overwhelmed. I never know just what I might hear on the other end of the line:

"Hi Vickie, I'm trying to find people to cook meals for the Johnsons this week, because Kathy is having surgery. When can I pencil you in?"

"We're having a class on making photo albums next Tuesday—can you come?"

"Vickie, it's Sally. Mike wanted to know if you can go with him to a conference in Texas this April."

"I just wanted to remind you that our Women's Ministries meeting is this Friday. Could you e-mail those agendas out to everyone?"

"I'm considering home schooling this year. Can you meet with me to tell me everything I need to know?"

"It's been ages since we've talked! How about lunch next week?"

Sometimes I feel that if I did not have to sleep, maybe then I could say yes to everything I am asked to do. Unfortunately, I and many others find it rather difficult to say no. We home schooling moms seem especially susceptible to taking on too many projects.

For one thing, some people automatically assume that stay-at-home moms have more time than those who work regular jobs. Thus, we are often the first to be asked to cook a meal, take on a new church project, or babysit someone's children.

However, some of us take on too many projects in and of our own free will. It can be constraining to feel that all we ever do is stay home and mind the children. We want a new challenge or a chance to use our hidden talents or a way to escape the home for a while. While it certainly is not wrong to want any of these things, they can become a trap to us if they distract us from our highest priorities.

So just what are our highest priorities? Simply put, they are the tasks that God has specifically given us to do. For those of us who have children, especially young ones, we need to realize that our primary assignment at this time in our lives is to care for our families. It is easy to think that other things are more important than just staying home, teaching our children, and making our house a home. Chapter 11 discusses the value of motherhood and why it is worth the sacrifice of career, ambition, or outside ministry. But for now, I just want to encourage you that God gives each of us different seasons of life in which to accomplish different tasks for Him. When you have young children, God's primary assignment for you is in the home. When they are grown and gone, He will have other jobs for you to do. But there are certain things we can and should do to serve others even now. When approached with a new job or project, do we automatically take it to prayer and determine whether or not it is something God would have us do? Or do we simply act on the spur of the moment, and under the influence of our current emotions?

Over the years, I have learned (often from my mistakes) how vital it is to seek God regarding how we should serve Him. As I studied the Scriptures to find out just how Jesus made the best use of His time, I discovered that Jesus always kept His focus on God's will and His priorities. When questioned about His actions, Jesus told the Jewish religious leaders, "Truly, truly, I say to you, the Son can do nothing of Himself, unless it is something He sees the Father doing; for whatever the Father does, these things the Son also does in like manner....I can do nothing on My own initiative, as I hear, I judge; and My judgment is just, because I do not seek My own will but the will of Him who sent Me" (John 5:19, 30).

Jesus was on earth to accomplish God's objectives, not His own. This meant that He knew what God wanted Him to do, and He did just that—no more, and no less.

In John 11, we read of a time when Jesus learned that His dear friend Lazarus, the brother of Mary and Martha, was gravely ill. Jesus and His disciples were in Jerusalem at the time, a mere two miles from Lazarus' home in Bethany. Nevertheless, Jesus stayed where He was for two days, until Lazarus had already died.

I wonder what Jesus' human reaction to Lazarus' illness must have been. I feel sure that He probably wanted to rush right to Bethany, heal Lazarus, and comfort Mary and Martha. But He knew that God had another plan. As He told His disciples, "This sickness is not unto death, but for the glory of God, that the Son of God may be glorified by it" (John 11:4). Jesus kept His focus on God's priorities, even when it meant saying no to His own emotions. For us, this may mean saying no to something that we really want to do. Or it may mean saying yes to something that frightens us. These decisions are never easy, and they may not please everyone. It must have been hard for Jesus to see Mary and Martha's sorrow, and to hear them say, "Lord, if only you had been here, my brother would not have died." But Jesus wanted to please His Father more than anyone else.

How did Jesus know what the Father wanted Him to be doing? According to the verse above in John, He did whatever He saw the Father doing. This meant that He was spending time with the Father, keeping His eyes on the Father, and watching the Father's every move. We come to know God's assignments for us simply by spending time with Him. So it is that we see a continued "upward spiral" when we decide to focus on only those tasks that God has given us. First, clearing away unnecessary projects frees up more time to spend with the Lord. Then, as we spend more time with Him, we can see Him and His will for us even more clearly.

My heart's desire is to be doing only those things that God wants me to be doing. I want to be "making the most of [my] time, because the days are evil" (Ephesians 5:16). I do not want my days sprinkled with fruitless activities that will undoubtedly crowd out my moments with the Lord. As I seek to make God's priorities my priorities, my prayer is the prayer of the psalmist:

> So teach us to number our days,
> That we may present to Thee a heart of wisdom....
> Let Thy work appear to Thy servants,
> And Thy majesty to their children.
> And let the favor of the Lord our God be upon us;
> And do confirm for us the work of our hands;
> Yes, confirm the work of our hands.
>
> Psalm 90:12, 16-17

OBEDIENCE: LOVE IN ACTION

When Mike and I started home schooling in 1982, we knew only one other home schooling family in our area. One of their daughters had been Christy's best friend in first grade, and they decided to home school at the same time we did. Christy was delighted that her best friend was also staying home for school, and I was delighted to find another mom with whom I could share ideas, support, and encouragement. Our two families formed a sort of tiny support group. As happy as I was to know another home schooling mom, however, there were times when our "support group" seemed a little inconvenient to my schedule. My friend, whom I'll call Jan, was much more talkative and activity-oriented than I am. She was usually the one to call me on the telephone or to plan an outing together. While I usually enjoyed our contact very much, once in a while it came at a busy time. On several occasions I was just getting ready to correct schoolwork, or mop the floor, or go out with Mike, when Jan would call.

Eventually, both of us became more and more caught up in our children and our school schedules, and we talked to each other somewhat less frequently. But Jan still called from time to time, and we would have long conversations about our lives and activities. She told me that she had taken up tennis, and would often play with her husband's friend, who was also a tennis enthusiast. Throughout the course of several conversations, this friend of her husband's seemed to keep reemerging. While I felt vaguely uneasy about this, I certainly was far from being seriously alarmed. Then for several weeks, I did not hear from Jan. As I would go about my daily activities, I kept hearing the Holy Spirit prompting me, "Call Jan, Vickie. You need to call Jan."

"Okay, Lord, I will...just as soon as I finish this laundry." But after I had finished the laundry, the baby woke up from her nap earlier than expected. "Well, Lord, I'll call her tonight after dinner." But then Mike suggested walking to Baskin-Robbins for ice cream. "Tomorrow, God," I would say at the end of the day. "I'll call Jan tomorrow." Many tomorrows later, Mike got a call from Jan's husband. Jan was leaving him, and filing for divorce. She had "fallen in love" with his friend.

You can imagine how heartsick I was. I had clearly sensed God's prompting to do something as simple as calling my friend, but I had let busyness take priority over obedience. Although I knew Jan was responsible for her own actions, I also knew that God had wanted to use me, and I had not been usable. I learned the hard way that when God does give me specific direction—either through His Word or through the prompting of the Holy Spirit—I need to respond with instant obedience.

Obedience is love in action. Throughout the Bible, love is continually equated with obedience. "If you love Me, you will keep My commandments," Jesus told His disciples (John 14:15). In 1 John 5:3, we read, "For this is the love of God, that we keep His commandments; and His commandments are not burdensome." If we do not obey God, then according to Scripture, we really do not love Him.

Obedience is certainly something to take seriously. It is useless to discover God's agenda for us unless we follow it, and it is useless for us to declare our love for God if we do not demonstrate it. Do not forget, however, that for those who love God, "His commandments are not burdensome." There is abundant joy and rest to be found in loving and obeying our Lord.

COME UNTO ME...

Just a few years ago, Mike and I were both invited to speak at a home school convention in Kansas. Our twelve-month-old son, Peter, was still nursing at the time, so we took him along with us.

Unfortunately, we had to fly through Denver to Wichita at a time when the Midwest was plagued by severe thunderstorms. Our trip was a complete nightmare—from bumpy flights to holding patterns to a cancelled connecting flight to lost luggage. In the midst of it all, I had to care for a highly active one-year-old who did not like being cooped up for long periods of time.

You can imagine my mood when Mike and I finally pulled up to a hotel in Denver, Colorado, without our luggage. It was past everyone's bedtime, Peter was screaming, I was exhausted, and Mike was frustrated. The thought that I was supposed to be speaking on home schooling the next morning only added to my sour mood. I was in no frame of mind to give anyone advice on how to trust God and care for a large family! All I wanted right then was to sleep for a long, long time.

As we stumbled through the hotel lobby doors, the first thing that hit our frazzled ears was the sound of piano music. Mike walked up to the check-in desk, and I stood holding Peter a few yards away. I watched the man playing the hotel piano, thinking how strange it was

that a moderately inexpensive hotel should be employ-
ing a pianist at this hour of the night. What was that
tune he was playing? It was so familiar . . .

"What a fellowship, what a joy divine, leaning on the
everlasting arms! What a blessedness, what a peace is mine,
leaning on the everlasting arms! Leaning, leaning…"

Mike came walking back, holding the room key. Our
eyes met in amazement. "Vickie, do you recognize that
tune?" Mike asked. I nodded, and we both stood listening to the rest of the song, feeling an amazing sense of
peace and refreshment. We were tired and frustrated and
worn, but we could lean on God's everlasting arms and
be held secure.

As I walked past the piano and toward the elevators,
I stopped to thank the pianist. "I couldn't believe it when
I walked in and heard you playing that song," I told him.
"It was just what I needed to hear right now." The man
nodded. "It's so good to know we can lean on the ever-
lasting arms," he said. I am still halfway convinced that
God sent an angel to our hotel lobby in Denver that
night! God's everlasting arms are always open to us.
There we can find peace, rest, refreshment, and the
strength to do what He's asked of us. He promises, "But
they that wait upon the Lord shall renew their strength"
(Isaiah 40:31, KJV), and "Cast your burden upon the
LORD, and He will sustain you; He will never allow the
righteous to be shaken" (Psalm 55:22).

We hear so much in the home schooling community
about "home school burnout." Almost all of us who have
been home schooling for a number of years know at

least one family who "just couldn't take it anymore."
(The most drastic case I have seen was a mother who
home schooled only one day before calling it quits!)
Seminars, workshops, and entire books have been
devoted to the subject of solving this problem. How can
we home school moms avoid feeling too tired, stressed,
and frustrated to go on?

I believe the answer is very simple, but for many,
unexpected. Simply seeking God, and making time for
Him, is the way to find rest and refreshment. If you are
feeling weary and burdened, Jesus' invitation in
Matthew 11:28-30 is for you:

"Come to Me, all who are weary and heavy laden,
and I will give you rest. Take My yoke upon you, and
learn from Me, for I am gentle and humble in heart; and
you shall find rest for your souls. For My yoke is easy,
and My load is light."

This is my beloved, and this is my friend, O daughters of Jerusalem.

8

TO LOVE
AND TO CHERISH

Putting Your Husband
Second Only to the Lord

I distinctly remember a conversation I had at a home
school conference just a few years ago. After one of
my rare public speeches, I had made my exit into the
hallway to talk with a few of my fellow moms one-on-
one. For me, this is always the best part of attending a
home school conference. I had reached a lull in the flow
of conversation when a woman approached me, introduced herself, and abruptly began: "Mrs. Farris, I can't
talk to my husband."

Thinking she meant she could not find the time to talk with her husband, I started asking her about the possibilities of babysitters and weekend getaways. She looked at me for a moment and said, "No, you don't understand. I really just can't talk to my husband." She explained that whenever they were alone together, whether at home at night or driving in the car, any conversation they had took the form of an argument. To avoid conflict, they usually sat in sullen silence, both engaged in their own private worlds. It had been many long months since they had held a decent conversation.

I did not have the time or insight of a marriage counselor, nor was a convention hall the place to thoroughly discuss such a subject. However, I did tell this distraught woman what I could: "After your relationship with God, your marriage is your absolute top priority. You need to do whatever you can to get this problem resolved, right away. Whether it's going to marriage counseling, taking a trip together, or even cutting back on your home schooling for a while, you need to make the time and energy to focus on fixing your marriage."

She nodded, although her face registered some surprise at the mention of cutting back on home schooling. Given my husband's well-known home school advocacy, and the fact that I had just finished a speech on home education myself, it is probably not the first thing she expected to hear. However, I wanted to stress that her relationship with her husband was so important that it even took priority over her children, her home schooling, her housekeeping, or any other duty.

My impression is that most of us home school moms remember that we need to be spending regular time with the Lord, even if it is a struggle. However, because our children are with us all day long, and we are constantly focusing on their needs and dealing with their problems, we tend to forget about the very real needs of our husbands. After a day spent as moms, teachers, cooks, housekeepers, launderers, nurses, and chauffeurs, being enthusiastic wives and lovers is often the farthest thing from our minds. "I'm tired, and I want some time alone for once," we are tempted to think. "He's a big boy. He can take care of himself!" Other times we are just so spent that, even though we recognize our husbands' needs, we feel we just have no more to give.

When we spend all our energy on our children at the expense of our husbands, however, we have our priorities backward. Throughout Scripture, it is clear that God expects married women to place their husbands as second only to God in their lives. Marriage is the only human relationship that God describes as two people becoming "one flesh"—certainly the ultimate in closeness. Moreover, in 1 Corinthians 7, the apostle Paul describes marriage as such an all-consuming relationship that he advises those who can remain single to do so, in order to be more fully devoted to the Lord! This does not mean that God has a low opinion of marriage, but simply that He expects (even commands) us to devote ourselves to our husbands almost as completely as we devote ourselves to Him.

We also need to remember that when we place our children before our husbands, we are actually doing our children a disservice. A healthy marriage is the foundation of a healthy family, and it is the ultimate human security for a child. Your children might currently be at the stage where they complain or cry at the sight of the babysitter, but in the long run they will feel more loved if they see love between their parents, and they will be overwhelmingly grateful for your commitment to each other.

With these things in mind, then, let's do a little "check-up" on our own marriages, and talk about some ways to make them stronger.

Pop Quiz!

When I speak on the topic of marriage at home school conferences, I usually read through a little checklist to get the women thinking about their relationships with their husbands. I have to admit that every time I read this list of questions, there is something on it that convicts me. Ask yourself:

1. Do you make some time each day to focus on your husband alone, talking to him about his day, his needs, his joys and frustrations?
2. Do you focus on your role as a helpmeet, rather than thinking of your husband as someone to help you?
3. Do you communicate to him admiration and respect, and verbally praise and encourage him?

4. Do you try to learn more about the things that interest him, so you can more fully be a part of his world?
5. Do you encourage him in his role as leader of the family, and are you willing to follow him when he does lead?
6. Do the two of you go out by yourselves sometimes, even if it is just to a fast food restaurant for coffee?
7. Do you do your part to keep your sex life healthy, strong, and exciting?
8. Are you now so discouraged that you are ready to skip over the rest of this chapter?

If you are discouraged, you are certainly not alone. Although Mike and I have a strong marriage, it still is not easy for me to put these things into practice when I am tired from a full day of home schooling and a bit cranky after dealing with my kids' sin natures all day long.

The bad news is this: At the end of the day, we won't always feel like saying something nice to our husbands or being an exciting lover. But the good news is this: Our success in this area does not have to depend on us, our strength, or our feelings. God has promised us that He never calls us to something He will not give us the power to do—and He has certainly called us to meet the needs of our husbands. Paul says in Philippians 4:13, "I can do all things through Him who strengthens me." And 2 Corinthians 9:8 promises, "And God is able to make all grace abound to you, that always having all sufficiency in everything, you may have an abundance for every good deed."

We have no excuses to be selfish. At the same time, I believe that when we set aside our own needs and desires, we will find this selflessness to be surprisingly rewarding. I can remember many times when I was worn and discouraged after a day with the kids, but when I took time to listen to Mike and the challenges of his day, my perspective became more balanced and my problems no longer seemed quite so insurmountable. Mike very often comes home with interesting stories of meetings and conversations he has had with various people throughout the day. Simply immersing myself in his world for a while seems to take the edge off the difficulties I have faced during my day. My problems often seem to disappear when I am with Mike, focusing on him and just enjoying being with him.

I have also found that if I am willing to set aside my own troubles at times in order to encourage and minister to Mike when he especially needs it, he then has more emotional strength to lift me up when I am down. As Proverbs 11:25 says, "He who waters will himself be watered." And Mike can be a very wise and wonderful encourager! There have been many times when his words have refreshed me and given me new strength to keep going. I only hope I am able to do the same for him.

We do have challenging lives to live—both wives and husbands—but Jesus is there to refresh, strengthen, and empower each one of us. We need to remember as wives that our husbands face a tough world with many challenges, and they desperately need our encouragement and love. If we say, "I can't—I don't have anything left!"

we are essentially saying, "God can't." But He can and will give us the grace to do that which He has called us to do, if we rely on Him.

In the preceding chapter, we looked at the areas of fellowship, focus, and obedience in our walk with God. Let's see how each of those areas applies to the marriage relationship.

Fellowship: Making Time Just for Him

Have you ever gone to a high school class reunion, or had a chance to chat with a long-lost childhood friend? As fun as it is to see someone from another time in your life, talk about life's changes, and relive old memories, it has been my experience that such conversations usually contain a bit of awkwardness. Except in unique cases, you and your old friend probably do not have the closeness that you once did. Perhaps you have gone completely separate ways and do not have much in common anymore. Whatever the reason, however, there is no denying that a friendship grows weak from a lack of communication and time spent together. A relationship based on ancient history alone is not a very strong one.

The sad fact is that the same thing can happen in our marriages. Perhaps this is what happened to the home schooling mother I mentioned at the beginning of the chapter, who had lost the ability to talk with her husband. Just like our fellowship time with the Lord, the time we spend with our husbands is absolutely invaluable. A relationship will certainly not grow, and may begin to die, if you do not spend time together.

Mike and I have had some days where most of our conversation was simply an exchange of information: "What time do I need to pick up the kids?"; "Where are you going on your business trip?"; "The church secretary needs you to call her right away." I can tell you from experience, however, that this kind of communication is not enough to keep a marriage thriving! Mike and I must make time to really talk to each other on a regular basis, sharing our thoughts and hearts, if our sense of "oneness" is to remain strong.

I must honestly admit that, while I truly desire that sense of oneness with Mike, I often find myself so distracted by my other duties that I fail to stop and really listen to him when he does talk to me. Just last night, as a matter of fact, he tried to share something with me, but I really could not concentrate on what he was saying amidst the hubbub of our household. He certainly understood my dilemma, but even when most of the kids are settled in bed, I tend to "putter" (as Mike calls it)—focusing on the laundry, the dishes, and the remaining items that need to be cleaned up. As a result, Mike sometimes has a hard time getting my attention.

There are times when he has had to say, "Vickie! Stop what you're doing and come sit on the couch next to me. I want to talk to you!" I have a very hard time sitting still when I am at home and I can see all the things that need to be done! While I have certainly honored Mike's request at those times and made myself sit down and listen, (and I have usually ended up enjoying that much more than my work!), what helps me the most is getting away from the house so I can give my complete attention to him. For this reason, we sometimes simply go to McDonald's or Wendy's just to be together and talk. Riding together in the car is also a good opportunity to talk, but what I enjoy the most is our walks. We share the happenings of the day, we discuss Mike's upcoming sermons and related theological issues, we solve problems we have been having with the kids, we chat back and forth, and I love it! It is a great time for us to really catch up with each other.

I also occasionally travel with Mike, and those times have proven to be wonderful relationship "boosters." Even when we have had a baby with us, we have still felt satisfyingly alone by comparison. Because I do not like to leave the kids very often, and it is usually a lot of work to prepare for these trips (I hate packing), I have sometimes had to force myself to go. But I know how important it is to Mike, and with both of our busy schedules, I know I need to take advantage of these special times with my husband. Besides, I usually end up enjoying myself tremendously once we get to our destination.

The foundation of my close fellowship with Mike is the simple fact that he has always been my very best friend. While I continue to maintain close friendships with several women, the person that I enjoy being with the most is Mike. I rarely go somewhere in the evenings without Mike, and even if I go shopping at the mall, he is my first pick for a partner. Likewise, Mike would rather be with me more than anyone else, and despite his busy schedule he consistently pursues opportunities for us to be together.

One of the key elements that has helped us to maintain such close fellowship is that Mike and I have determined to never let the sun go down on our anger. Just
as we need to confess our sins daily to the Lord and
keep a "clean slate" in order to maintain fellowship with
Him, it is vital to deal immediately with any issues that
are hindering close fellowship with our husbands.
There is nothing worse than going through the day with
unresolved anger burning between Mike and me. That
has happened at times, and I absolutely hate it! As much
as possible, Mike and I try to deal with the trouble at
hand as quickly as we can. We have been known to stay
up until 3:00 or 4:00 A.M. in order to solve a disagree-
ment, so that we can truly be "one" again in spirit and
flesh. And Mike knows how important it is to me to
have a oneness in spirit before I can enjoy oneness in
the flesh, so he is usually highly motivated to resolve
our disagreements!

Indeed, physical intimacy and "oneness in the flesh"
are absolutely vital parts of your fellowship with your
husband. If you find that you are too tired or emotionally stressed to meet this fundamental need for your
husband, I believe you need to consider dropping out of
other activities so you can be more enthusiastically
available to him. Sexual intimacy is a precious gift from
God, and it sets the marriage relationship apart in its
complete unity and openness. Of all God's precious
gifts, this is the one your husband can legitimately share
with no human being on earth besides you. Of all your
husband's needs, this is the one that only you have the

right and privilege to meet. Furthermore, of all his needs, this is the one that should never be set aside. There are too many women out there who are willing to pick up your slack, and even godly Christian men can fall. You can be a very effective antidote to temptation, and I guarantee your husband will appreciate it tremendously, if you show interest in him physically and delight in your physical relationship with him.

God looked at Adam and said, "It is not good for man to be alone." His solution was to create Eve as Adam's helpmeet and partner. We need to remember that, even today, our first duty is to be our husbands' partners and companions in life. Since marriage was clearly created to include intimate fellowship, what a tragedy it would be to allow our marriages to become little more than working relationships!

Focus: Pleasing Him First

In the last chapter, we talked about the importance of maintaining a focus on the Lord and His priorities. Although this idea of "focus" has a somewhat different application in our marriage relationships, there are four specific areas upon which I believe we wives would do well to focus in regard to our husbands.

First, focus on your husband's interests and desires. If you are like most couples, you and your husband probably share many of the same interests and desires, and your similar goals will cause you to work together more naturally. However, I believe that many men have at least a few interests that their wives either do not share or perhaps even dislike. If your husband has interests and desires that do not particularly excite you, one of the most meaningful things you could do for him would be to educate yourself in those areas and become interested for his sake. He wants you to be a part of his world!

Although my least favorite subjects in school were politics and government, ironically, God chose to give me a husband who is actively involved in politics, law, and public policy. Early on, it was important for me to educate myself in these areas in order to truly be a part of Mike's world. This was fortunately not as difficult as I might have anticipated, since Mike's involvement and enthusiasm made the political process come alive for me.

However, there are certain aspects about Mike's work that I have had to work a little harder to truly appreciate. One of those areas is attending the various functions, picnics, banquets, and other gatherings that are the lifeblood of insider politics. I am naturally shy, and the prospect of spending an evening making small talk with complete strangers has never been an exciting one. Over the years, however, I have realized the importance of sharing in the activities that play so much of a role in my husband's life work. Even if I still do not enjoy a political dinner as much as I enjoy a long walk, I have learned to appreciate such an evening for the insight it gives me into Mike.

For Mike's birthday this year, I spent the day on the golf course with him. Golf has become his favorite recreational activity, and he is very pleased when I get the rare opportunity to golf with him. Although I naturally enjoy the chance to be outdoors, it is often hard for me to justify spending three hours golfing when I have so much else to do. However, I try to golf with Mike as often as I can, being his partner in fun as well as in work.

Second, focus on pleasing your husband over your children, your friends, and yourself. Often it is the little sacrifices that are the most difficult to make, but they speak volumes when you do make them. Don't go to that Mom's Night Out if your husband was hoping to spend the evening with you. Wear that dress he especially likes, even if you do not really feel like getting dressed up.

"Love seeks not its own," God tells us in the classic passage on love, 1 Corinthians 13. This concept of self-sacrifice is anathema to the world around us, who see love as merely an exhilarating feeling, an emotional high that makes us feel good about ourselves. "It's your life, and it's your body," the world tells us. "Don't be a doormat." But God's Word tells us something quite different: "The wife does not have authority over her own body, but the husband does; and likewise also the husband does not have authority over his own body, but the wife does" (1 Corinthians 7:4). When you put your husband's desires above your own, you are demonstrating true love as Christ defined it by His own example.

Third, focus on your husband's good qualities, and make sure you tell him about them. I have learned from my own mistakes how crucial it is to be my husband's biggest fan. This has been one of my areas of weakness, and I have really had to work on learning to tell Mike the ways in which I admire him. Even though I often notice admirable qualities in his character and actions, I have sometimes had a hard time verbalizing my admiration! Nevertheless, verbal praise is something that is very important to Mike, and I have gradually learned to use it—even though it did not come naturally at first. Mike works in an arena where he hears both praise and criticism often. When he travels to home school conferences, he often speaks with families who greatly admire and appreciate the work he has done to further home education. When he attends political functions, he is often recognized for his achievements. However, he has told me many times that nothing is more meaningful to him than praise from me.

Just as our praise can be especially meaningful to our husbands, so our criticism can be especially devastating. Although our husbands certainly have their faults, we can choose whether to focus on the positive or on the negative. We need to try hard not to focus on the negative. I have set a goal for myself to look for something that I can admire or praise Mike for every day, and then I try to be sure to tell him. Words can be powerful tools to either build or destroy relationships. Set a goal for yourself to use words to strengthen your marriage.

Fourth, focus on the unique way your husband expresses love—his "love language." After nearly thirty years of marriage, I rarely feel the need to read "marriage manuals." However, just after my oldest daughter Christy left for her honeymoon, I found a book on our dining room table that she had received as an early wedding gift. Its title intrigued me: *The Five Love Languages,* by Gary Chapman. I began to read, and by the time I had reached the second chapter I was thinking, "I wish this book had been around when I got married!"

The Five Love Languages explores the concept that each of us expresses and receives love in an individual way: through words of appreciation, acts of service, giving and receiving gifts, quality time, or physical touch. Chapman thoroughly defines each of these love languages and explains that the way we express love is usually the way we want to receive it. Unfortunately, many of us speak a different love language than our spouse does, and much miscommunication occurs.

At first, I thought that my husband's love language must be physical touch, and I suspect that many women would think the same thing about their husbands. However, as I read further, I realized that his love language was actually words of appreciation. He feels most loved when I verbally express my admiration for him, and he is most hurt when I fail to praise him, or when I verbally tear him down.

For many years, I tried showing Mike that I loved him by spending quality time with him and providing various acts of service. Unfortunately, all my efforts to set aside time just for him and to provide him with a neat home, clean clothes, and warm meals were not as effective in expressing my love as a simple word of praise would have been. Although I essentially discovered the concept of "love languages" by trial and error, I wish I had been told earlier in my marriage how to express love to Mike in a way that he would understand it.

I encourage you to make a thorough study of your husband to discover just how he best expresses and receives love. Learning to speak my husband's love language certainly improved my marriage, even after so many happy years.

SUBMISSION: ALLOWING HIM TO LEAD

I was in the process of preparing a speech called "The Top Two Priorities of a Home Schooling Mom," on the subject of a woman's relationship with both God and her husband, when I learned an interesting lesson in submission.

It was the middle of the school year, and my son Michael was struggling with his math. Day after day I would become frustrated with him, as he failed to grasp concepts that we had drilled repeatedly. As I took a walk with Mike one evening, I launched into a long complaint about my struggles with Michael's math. I mentioned a solution that I had in mind, and asked Mike what he thought about it. Instead of agreeing with my idea, or at least refining it, Mike offered a completely different solution. To be honest, it was an idea that I just did not like at all. I did not feel like putting it into practice, and besides, I was sure that it would not work. Basically dismissing it without a second thought, I went back to discussing the merits of my idea. Although Mike brought up his solution several more times, I was not even considering it as an option.

Suddenly, Mike stopped walking. I looked back at him, surprised. "Vickie," he said, now that he had gotten my attention, "does it seem to you that whenever I've asked you to do something lately, you've just totally ignored me? I seriously think this is what you should do. Why aren't you listening to me?" I was cut to the quick. "Oh my goodness, he's right!" I realized. "I have been dismissing Mike's requests lately! Here I am, preparing to give a speech on the importance of loving and submitting to my husband, and I'm not even doing it myself!" It was a very humbling realization indeed!

I immediately apologized to Mike and put his suggestion into practice the next day. To my surprise, it worked just as he had predicted! And I was able to give my speech, using this incident as an example of what not to do.

By drawing a correlation between our obedience to God and our submission to our husbands, I am not suggesting that our husbands have the same authority as the Holy Spirit does in our lives. I certainly believe that wives have the right to express their perspective and to respectfully appeal decisions. There have been many times when Mike has sought my advice, and he has always taken my opinion seriously. However, if your husband makes a final decision, you need to willingly follow—even if you do not like it.

Sometimes it is hard for us to believe that God is speaking and acting through our fallible husbands. However, as in the situation with Michael's math, this is often exactly what He does. He has set up husbands and fathers as the heads of families, and I believe that He primarily directs families through these men. In Ephesians 5:22-24, we read:

Wives, be subject to your own husbands, as to the Lord. For the husband is the head of the wife, as Christ also is the head of the church, He Himself being the Savior of the body. But as the church is subject to Christ, so also the wives ought to be to their husbands in everything.

God has set up certain authority structures through which He speaks and acts. He commands children to be subject to their parents, wives to be subject to their husbands, and citizens to be subject to their governments. When we disobey or dishonor the authority over us, He sees it as disobedience to Him.

One thing I have noticed is that no verse in Scripture says, "Husbands, force your wives to submit to you." Rather, the Scriptures' commandment is directed to the wives. It is our responsibility as wives to submit to our husbands voluntarily and willingly, in obedience to the Lord.

THE SPECIAL CHALLENGE
OF A BUSY HUSBAND

Late one night, I sat in the kitchen in my pajamas, enjoying a rare chance to read a magazine. A glance at the clock told me it was 12:30 A.M., so I knew Mike should be home any minute now. Just forty minutes earlier he had called me on his cell phone to tell me he had arrived safely at Dulles Airport.

Sure enough, I heard his step on the back porch a minute later. He walked in the door, set his suitcase down with a tired thud, and greeted me with a kiss. "Oh, I have something for you," he said, rummaging through one of his bags. He pulled out a lovely basket of home-made preserves, candies, and baked goods, along with a card addressed to "Mrs. Farris."

"Dear Vickie," the card read, "thank you for your sacrifice in lending your husband to us and to the home schooling movement. We greatly appreciate the work he is doing on our behalf, and we thank you for the work you are doing to support him and raise those ten children. May God bless you!" The card was signed by the home school leaders at whose convention Mike had just spoken. I am always surprised by such thoughtfulness, even though Mike often comes home bearing cards, gifts, and words of appreciation for me from people I have never met. The thing that encourages me most is not so much the recognition of my sacrifice, but rather the knowledge that the sacrifice is indeed worthwhile—that it is impacting the lives of others.

I use the word "sacrifice," because I cannot deny that it is difficult at times to have such a busy husband. His work requires him to be on the road an average of seven nights a month, more frequently during the busy home school conference season. And then there was 1993, the year that he ran for lieutenant governor of Virginia with my full blessing and approval. During that time, he was away from home for the better part of a year.

Mike's travel schedule is not the only thing that keeps him busy. His regular responsibilities as president of HSLDA, elder and interim pastor for our church, president of Patrick Henry College, executive producer of a home school website, author, and political activist keep him hopping even when he is home.

Without a doubt, this very active lifestyle has been one of the unique challenges of our marriage, and it has kept me doubly dependent on the Lord for strength. When Mike is gone, I must assume the full "on-site" responsibility for the household. This means that, for a short time, I am the one who handles family decisions, tough discipline cases, and plumbing problems.

One of most difficult aspects of taking on this responsibility is that I must continually adapt from being in charge to being in submission. I tend to get used to being the final authority in the house, and when Mike returns from a long trip it is sometimes hard to hand the reins over again. I believe this can be a challenge for many women—even if the extent of your husband's travel is his daily commute to work. Making that evening transition from being the authority to being under authority can cause some tension in the marriage relationship.

I need to watch my attitude in this area not only when Mike gets home, but also while he is still away. I find that by maintaining a submissive attitude throughout the day, remembering that Mike is still the authority, and continuing to uphold his commands and desires for the household in his absence, it is much easier to submit again upon his return. If upon Mike's departure I immediately think, "Okay, I'm in charge now, and I'm going to runs things my way!" you can bet

I'll be having some problems submitting when he gets home! In addition, when I honor Mike's wishes and desires in his absence, I myself feel less weighed down by the burden of authority.

The simple fact that Mike and I are apart so often is another challenge in keeping our relationship strong and healthy. One important thing that keeps me going when Mike is away is the fact that he always calls me every night, whether he is in Kansas City or Moscow. As I mentioned before, Mike is generally better at making time to talk than I am, and it is no different when his schedule is incredibly demanding. Even when he is not traveling, he often calls me during the day just to "check in," see how I am doing, and let me know he is thinking of me.

Also, Mike often returns from his trips with little gifts (or sometimes not-so-little gifts) that he buys for me on the road. Like his frequent phone calls, these gifts show me that Mike is thinking of me while he is away. It means a great deal just to know he is with me in spirit, if not in body!

Another thing that keeps Mike and me close, despite his busy travel schedule, is that I'll occasionally travel with him. As I mentioned earlier, I sometimes have to force myself to pack my bags, leave the house and children, and go. Once I do, however, I find the time with Mike to be very refreshing for both of us. It is also a good chance for me to meet the people with whom he spends so much time, once again becoming more fully a part of his world.

When I am not able to travel with Mike, I have to consciously make it a priority to spend time with him once he gets home. We will often try to go out together shortly after he gets back from a trip, and I have learned to drop whatever else is going on in order to free up this important time for my husband. I appreciate the fact that Mike takes the leadership in this area and is always looking for small ways to share fellowship with me.

Although each of these practical measures helps keep my marriage strong through the challenges, the thing that truly means the most is the knowledge that Mike is doing important work for the Lord, and that I am a part of it. That is why I am so encouraged to receive notes from the people who are blessed by Mike's work and travel—it lets me know that my sacrifice is worthwhile.

When Mike entered law school, I was somewhat skeptical that he could ever use a law degree to further God's kingdom. I just did not see how God could use a lawyer for His purposes! Nevertheless, I began praying in faith that God would do just that. Over the years, it has truly been a joy to see that prayer answered more abundantly than I could ever have dreamed. Although sometimes this means more work for me, or a few lonely nights, the knowledge that Mike and I are partners in ministry is certainly worth the sacrifice.

Wherever God is using your husband, know that you have a vital place in his work and life as an encourager, helpmeet, partner, and friend. As you make the time and effort to put him first, you will find your own needs and desires fulfilled in ways you could not have imagined.

"Make my joy complete by being of the same mind, maintaining the same love, united in spirit, intent on one purpose" (Philippians 2:2).

It is vain for you to rise up early, to sit up late, to eat the bread of sorrows; for so He gives His beloved sleep.

PSALM 127:2, NKJV

9

WHEN DO I
GET A COFFEE
BREAK?

Time for Yourself

I t was a relatively quiet Saturday afternoon. The house
was finally clean, and I was a woman on a mission: I
wanted to make a phone call. (And if you're a busy
mom, you know that can be Mission: Impossible!) I had
been meaning to call my friend Jeanne for the past several days, and I decided now was as good a time as any.

I had just retreated to my bedroom and picked up
the receiver when I heard the knock of a little fist on my
door. "Mom," my son Joseph called, "can I go over to
play at Megan's house?"

Oh, good, this was an easy one. "Yes, Joe," I replied, dialing the number. But just as the phone began ringing, I had another visitor: my daughter Emily.

"Mom! Michael threw a shoe at me for no reason!"

"Hold on a minute, Emily. Hi, Jeanne? This is Vickie...hi...doing fine...I'm sorry it took so long to call you back. Listen, could you hold on for just a minute? I need to take care of this problem here."

I quickly dealt with the issue of shoe-throwing and returned to my conversation. Two minutes later, however, Peter shuffled into my room, his hair freshly rumpled from his nap and his eyes full of sleep and tears. "Mo-o-o-mm," he wailed, "I want juice in my bottle!"

Jessica quickly came to my rescue, taking Peter downstairs for his bottle. However, just as Peter's crying subsided, I could hear the back door open to let in the frantic sound of Jonathan sobbing. "I fell off my bike!" he tearfully announced to everyone within earshot, which was just about the whole house.

And so it continued. Finally, after about fifteen minutes of constantly interrupted conversation, Jeanne and I decided to give up and try again at a better time. I sighed as I hung up the telephone, wondering just when that better time would be. Interruptions, it seems, are an inevitable part of life.

I would guess that just about every mother of young children knows the frustration of constant interruptions. You're just sitting down to read a magazine article when you hear a loud thud and a frantic cry for "Mom!" You're trying to concentrate on preparing a Bible study devotional when a dirty diaper demands your attention, or a fight breaks out, or someone can't find his baseball glove. On some days I can't even go to the bathroom without someone calling for me or knocking on the bathroom door!

"Why is it that Mike can concentrate on getting his things done, but I can't?" I am often tempted to think. "After all, they're his kids too, aren't they? When am I ever going to get some time for myself?"

Besides envying our husbands, it is sometimes tempting to envy other women who seem to have more free time than we do. There have been several occasions when Mike and I attended a political dinner and were seated at a table with several couples around our age. I remember being struck with how different my life is compared with most women of my generation. With most of their children grown, these women are now focused on jobs, charity involvement, hobbies, and travel. When they talk about their children, the conversations center on colleges, weddings, and grandchildren. While I can relate to these topics, I am also still very much in the world of diapers, bottles, and school assignments. I sometimes wonder what it would be like to have my work essentially finished, and to have time to do lunch with friends or take up oil painting. For heaven's sake, I'd just like a chance to read a good book every once in a while!

When Christy and Jayme were young, I always looked forward to their daily naptime as "my time." The house was quiet, and I was essentially free to do whatever I wanted: read a book, take a nap, write a letter, or spend some time with the Lord. As Christy began to get too old for naps, my free time began disappearing. But I was not worried—I knew she would soon be going to school, and I would have time for myself again. When we decided to home school, however, everything changed. Not only did I have the added responsibility of teaching, but I also had no quiet time for myself anymore. My schedule became even more demanding as our family grew with each new baby.

Around that time, I remember coming to the conclusion that I was going to have to change my outlook on free time. I consciously realized that, if I was to follow this life of home schooling and having many children, I was simply going to get less time for myself. I also realized that I could either choose to be discontent and demand my "right" to free time, or I could choose to die to my "rights" and be content. I decided the latter was the better option!

As revolutionary as this may sound, it does not mean that I never get time for myself. The Lord has been good to provide me with rest and refreshment when I needed it most. However, I simply have given up the idea that I am entitled to free time. Instead, I have chosen to look to God to provide this need for me, as He has abundantly provided for every other need in my life. Believe it or not, I have found that by dying to self and giving up my "rights," I have actually gained much more than I have given up.

HE WHO LOSES HIS LIFE WILL GAIN IT

"Wait a minute," you might be thinking. "Is she saying that if I have a large family and home school them, I'll have to give up all my free time? I don't think I'm ready for that. How can anyone ask me to give up time for myself?"

I'll be perfectly straightforward: a decision to have many children and to home school them does not mean you will never have time for yourself again, but it does mean you will have to make certain sacrifices. If you have made your decisions about family size and education based on Scripture, then carrying out those decisions is a matter of obedience to God. And God has never been hesitant to let people know that following Him involves a cost.

Jesus could never have been accused of false or "slick" advertising when he invited people to be His disciples. Rather, He was completely honest about the cost of following Him:

> And He summoned the multitude with His disciples, and said to them, "If anyone wishes to come after Me, let him deny himself, and take up his cross, and follow Me. For whoever wishes to save his life shall lose it; but whoever loses his life for My sake and the gospel's shall save it. For what does it profit a man to gain the whole world, and forfeit his soul?" (Mark 8:34-36)

On another occasion, Jesus advised people to thoroughly consider the cost before embarking on a life of discipleship:

> "For which one of you, when he wants to build a tower, does not first sit down and calculate the cost, to see if he has enough to complete it? Otherwise, when he has laid a foundation, and is

not able to finish, all who observe it begin to ridicule him, saying, 'This man began to build and was not able to finish.' Or what king, when he sets out to meet another king in battle, will not first sit down and take counsel whether he is strong enough with ten thousand men to encounter the one coming against him with twenty thousand? Or else, while the other is still far away, he sends a delegation and asks terms of peace. So therefore, no one of you can be My disciple who does not give up all his own possessions." (Luke 14:28-33)

By the world's standards, the kingdom of God is utterly upside-down and inside-out. Those who would be great must be servants. Those who want to gain their lives must give them up. The first are last and the last first; the rich are poor and the poor rich. If we are seeking a life of ease and relaxation—"the path of least resistance"—then we must ask ourselves just why we are following Jesus anyway. He has already made it clear that the Christian life is one of servanthood.

What does this mean in my everyday life? It is essentially an attitude adjustment: I try to remember that my time is not really mine, but rather the Lord's. When I don't get the time to read a magazine or make a phone call, I should have no basis for complaint—because that time is not mine to claim. When I do get a little time to relax, however, I should receive it with thanksgiving as an undeserved gift from God.

Although Jesus said that this self-denial was a prerequisite for any disciple of His, I believe we mothers have the unique opportunity to really practice "taking up our crosses" and following Him. With little ones utterly dependent on us, we have a special chance to model God's self-giving love for His children. Remember that with greater "freedom" comes greater temptation to live for our own pleasure. Rather than complaining about your current situation, or envying those who do not have small children, rejoice that your life naturally compels you to the kind of service to which God calls each of us!

It was years ago when I first "counted the cost" of this lifestyle and made the conscious decision to give up all my rights to my own time. However, I have discovered since then that dying to self is a daily process! Every day I face the choice to complain or rejoice, especially when I am tired or the kids are unusually demanding. When I tried to reclaim my rights and just whine is when I needed to focus on the fact that I am not "giving up my life" just for the sake of losing it, but for the sake of gaining it. When I give up my own rights and my own life, I gain abundant blessing in return.

WORKING FOR HIDDEN TREASURE

I love the parable Jesus told about a man who found a treasure hidden in a field. Telling no one of his find, the man quickly reburied the treasure, and then he left in excitement and haste to purchase the field. It was an expensive piece of land—he had to sell all that he had in order to buy it. Perhaps his friends and family thought he was crazy to sell all his possessions to buy a simple field. But the man would not be dissuaded—he knew the field was more valuable than it seemed. As soon as he possessed it, great wealth would be his.

Jesus said the Kingdom of God was like that hidden treasure. We must give up much (sometimes all) in order to possess it. Perhaps it looks as if we are not gaining much in return. But the reality is that we are giving up something of far less value than what we are gaining. The reward is well worth the price—and then some.

So it has been in my life. Although on a daily basis I may struggle with feeling tired or discouraged, in the long term I can honestly say I have gained much more than I have given up. Any lack of sleep or absence of peace and quiet I have experienced has been far, far outweighed by the joy my children have been to me. In fact, as I sat in my room contemplating these things, Peter bounded in and gave me several big, joyous bear hugs. There is nothing better than a sincere, loving hug from little Peter!

A few minutes later, Katie showed up with her new little daughter, Jenna. As I held my little granddaughter in my lap, I was struck again with the awe and wonder of human life and of the Creator who gives that life. I remembered looking into the faces of my own babies and feeling such a strong sense of God's presence in these miraculous little gifts from heaven. It was a feeling that is hard now to describe, but I would not trade the memory of it for anything!

All the adoring smiles from my infants, the antics of my toddlers, and the special pictures drawn just for me by my young children have been more than enough payment for the energy expended in caring for and teaching these little ones. And there is just something about young children and their excitement about life that refreshes and invigorates me, no matter how tired I am.

The movies I have missed; the magazines and books that have gone unread; get-togethers, lunches, and Bible studies I could not attend; shopping trips I have had to say no to—all of these are an easy trade-in for the eternal rewards of loving children, close family relationships, character-building opportunities, and a godly heritage that will hopefully affect generations to come.

That is perhaps the greatest reward of all: to be able to see your grown children walking with the Lord and in turn beginning godly families of their own. The apostle John's words in 3 John 4 are so true: "I have no greater joy than this, to hear of my children walking in the truth." And that is worth any sacrifice!

BUT WHAT *CAN* I DO WHEN I'M TIRED?

So does all this mean that it is wrong to ever have any time for ourselves? Should we use every available minute as a chance to work? Should we run ourselves ragged and never get any rest? Should we feel guilty for taking small breaks to read a book or call a friend? Of course not. With the truth that the Christian life is one of service comes the balancing truth that we were designed to need rest, and we will not be able to serve anyone if we do not take care of that need. I believe that "dying to ourselves" is something that needs to take place in our hearts and minds—it is a mindset, a heart attitude. In daily life and practice, taking time for ourselves is something we will need to do from time to time, in order to "recharge the batteries" and keep serving.

Our time is to be the Lord's—but when the Lord was setting up a schedule for the nation of Israel, He ordained an entire day for rest from work. Obviously, yielding our time to God's control will not preclude all rest or refreshment. Although the Lord was the one who ordained the Sabbath day, you'll notice that He did not physically force the people to rest or magically make all their work go away for that day. Rather, on the day before the Sabbath the people were supposed to prepare to rest, doing any necessary work ahead of time. Then it was their duty to actively set aside that day as a time for rest and reflection on the Lord. In the same way, there will be times when we will deliberately have to make the time for an emotional or physical break.

If you are like me, oftentimes you need an emotional break even more than a physical one. Just getting out of the house, or taking your mind off your duties for a while, can prove to be surprisingly refreshing. Although most of us probably will not be able to spend a day at the spa or take off on a Caribbean cruise, there are many ways that even the busiest of home school moms can provide themselves with an emotional break.

My solution for an emotional, spiritual, and physical break is my daily walk. I fight for that four-mile walk every day—maybe I fight a little too hard at times! This is basically the only free time I have, but it is all I really need to keep going. I love the outdoors, and it is amazing what a little fresh air and sunshine can do for your outlook on life. We live out in the country in Loudoun County, Virginia, and I thoroughly enjoy the quiet and beauty of the countryside as I walk. Besides providing me with a chance to get out of the house for an hour, it also helps me stay fit and healthy—which is important both for me and for my husband.

Whenever Mike and I plan our school schedule for the year, "Mom's walk" is one of the permanent items in the daily plan. I usually get out for my walk in the afternoon, after school is finished and before I start making dinner. If we are running late, I'll often postpone my walk until after dinner—if it's dark, Mike or one of the kids will join me. Two years ago we bought a treadmill for those times when bad weather, darkness, or lack of a walking partner would keep me from my daily exercise. In this way, I am able to stay flexible about the timing of the walk, but still use a little of my God-given time to take care of my body and get a break!

Another way that I relax or get away is by going to lunch with a friend. Although I do not do this very often, I do enjoy these rare chances for one-on-one conversation in the luxury of a quiet setting. Mike and I also get away once in a while for dinner, even if it's only fast food.

For many years now, my friend Linda has had a regularly-scheduled "date night" with her husband. No matter what else is on the schedule, Bill and Linda go out together every Friday night, despite (or maybe because of) the fact that they have eleven children! Mike and I have also done this occasionally, especially after I had just had a new baby. I often would get "cabin fever" in the weeks following a new birth, because I had been home so long attending to the new little one. After Michael was born, Mike and I went to Wendy's every

Sunday night with the new baby in tow. It became our little tradition, and it helped me get out of the house. After Peter's birth, we would sometimes rent a movie, take baby Peter with us, and go over to watch the movie at Mike's office, just as another chance for a low-budget evening getaway.

When I don't have much time at my disposal but need a quick break, I often enjoy reading little snatches of *Reader's Digest*, *World*, or the *Washington Times*. I also play the piano, and once in a while I'll retreat to our living room just to play for a little while. Sometimes a few minutes of emotional escape are all I need to recharge my batteries.

Although I have never really gotten involved in support group activities (otherwise it is just too hard for me to keep things going at home), other moms have found home school support groups to be a wonderful source of refreshment. Many support groups hold events like "Mom's Night Out" or "Park Day," which give both kids and moms a chance to socialize. I have known other home schooling moms who have done the same thing on a smaller scale—two moms would get together for a "kid trade." One of the women would watch all the children while the other ran errands, corrected schoolwork, or did something fun. They would then switch off—providing each mom with a little time for herself.

Besides emotional fatigue, home schooling moms can also deal with very real physical fatigue. Our bodies do need enough sleep, proper nutrition, and some exercise, and here again we will not be very good wives or mothers if we are stretched to the limit—emotionally or physically. But in the pressure of our busy lives, sleep or exercise often seems to be the first thing to go!

The area of sleep is a sensitive subject for many of us. I saw this clearly when I hosted an online chat for a group of home schooling mothers a few months ago. One of the first things I was asked was, "Vickie, what time do you wake up in the morning?" I have to admit that I avoided the subject until my friend Geni, who was monitoring the chat session, sent me a private instant message saying: "Please tell them, Vickie, it will be encouraging for many!" Once I finally confessed that I often wake up at 8:30 or 9:00, the chat room erupted with the electronic exclamations of fellow late-sleepers who felt a little better about their sleeping schedules.

The truth is that I don't think it's wise to run myself ragged attempting to follow a man-made standard of diligence or good motherhood. In my case, I do not function very well if I do not get an average of eight hours of sleep a night. I also generally tend to be a night-owl, getting a lot accomplished after the children have gone to bed, and then sleeping a little later in the morning. However, I know many women who keep very different schedules. The most extreme case is one mother who goes to bed at 8:00 P.M. and wakes at 2:00 A.M., having her "free time" from then until her children wake up. This schedule works perfectly for her, but I could never do that.

I know we are tempted to think that those who wake up at 5:00 a.m. are somehow more "spiritual" than those who sleep later, but God designed each person differently. He holds each of us to a standard of faithfulness, orderliness, and diligence, but not to a specific schedule. If I am being faithful to complete the tasks God has given me each day, He will not frown on me for getting up at 8:30—even if others already have half their school day finished by that time!

I also know that I can only do so much with the energy I have, and I have learned over the years to go a little easy on myself when I can, despite what other people may think. That is why, though I resisted for years, I do employ a cleaning lady once a week, and that has proven to be an incredible blessing. I just don't know how I would ever have any free time without that extra help.

Also, we eat simple meals for breakfast and lunch, with most of the kids getting the food themselves. Yes, this usually means cold cereal instead of eggs and toast, and hot pockets or macaroni and cheese more often than homemade soup and sandwiches, but I know I would go crazy if I tried to be "The Perfect Mom" in everything. I would like to spend more time planning more gourmet meals when I am able to, but for now I can just barely handle making a good, healthy dinner every night. And (true confessions here) we usually use paper plates at most of our meals, too. It really makes cleanup a lot easier, and every little bit helps.

Despite what the rest of the family sometimes eats, however, I do try to keep myself on a diet that consists mostly of proteins, fruits, and vegetables. I have found that I can keep my weight where I want it if I avoid starches as much as possible. I do still allow myself some dessert every day, however—I have an incurable sweet tooth and it is just too hard for me to give up dessert.

I have always worked very hard to get back into my pre-pregnancy clothing after I have had a baby, and I have always managed to do it. Whereas it used to take me just two months to lose all the weight I had gained, in my later pregnancies it took me at least six to nine months (remember, I was often pregnant again in eleven months, so I had to work fast!). I have found that I feel so much better physically and mentally when I work to stay fit and trim. I feel good about myself, which seems to affect every other area of my life. And Mike tells me constantly how much he appreciates my efforts.

On the subject of rest, free time, and emotional refreshment, one of the verses that has encouraged me (believe it or not) is Philippians 2:4. Paul says, "Do not merely look out for your own personal interests, but also for the interests of others." This verse provides us with a good balancing principle; it actually assumes that we will naturally attend to our own interests, but it also commands us to attend to the interests of others. When we have hearts of service, we will naturally want to serve others to the best of our ability. But this means that we ourselves will need to take some time—even if it is just a few minutes—to refresh ourselves for continued service.

Although as a home schooling mom you probably won't have entire afternoons or evenings at your disposal, I do encourage you to "open" those gifts of one hour, thirty minutes, or even ten minutes that God gives you. If you can't take a nap for two hours, maybe you can take a warm bath for thirty minutes. If you don't have the time for a long lunch with your friend, maybe you do have time for a fifteen-minute phone call, or perhaps your friend could come to your house for lunch. And when you do have a chance for a break, receive it not with a sense of guilt, nor with a sense of entitlement, but with simple gratitude to the God who cares for your every need.

My Expectation is from Him

We have seen in this chapter that there is a delicate line between demanding our own rights and simply making time to get rest and refreshment. How can we walk this line?

It is much easier for me to find the balance between service and rest when I look at Psalm 62:5. "My soul, wait thou only upon God; for my expectation is from him" (KJV). In other words, all we have belongs to the Lord, and all we need comes from the Lord. We are both to yield everything to God and expect everything from Him. When we consider our time as His, and not our own, we can also look to Him to provide our need for rest and refreshment.

In the Bible, we see many examples of the Lord providing rest to a weary servant just when he or she needed it most. Just after Elijah's incredible victory over the prophets of Baal on Mt. Carmel, he experienced a deep sense of discouragement and depression. He fled into the desert and prayed to die. God, rather than becoming angry with Elijah, sent an angel to minister to him. The angel allowed Elijah to sleep and then provided him with food, saying, "Arise, eat, because the journey is too great for you." (1 Kings 19:7). After Elijah had recovered physically, the Lord gently reassured him of His presence and of the fact that Elijah was not the only Israelite who had remained faithful to God. Immediately thereafter, the Lord provided Elijah with a helper—Elisha—who would eventually take over his ministry as prophet over Israel.

God knows our needs, just as He knew Elijah's needs. If we need physical strength, spiritual stamina, emotional encouragement, or human help, He will not fail to give it to us. Nor will He fault us if we bring our needs and requests before Him. In fact, there have been many times when I have seen this to be true in my own life. One day, just when I was at the breaking point, my friend Geni called to ask, "Can I take all your kids for the afternoon?" At other times, I had just hit bottom when a friend called to encourage me or someone invited me out to lunch or Mike came home unexpectedly to take the kids on an outing. God provided just when I needed it most.

The Lord wants us to look to Him as our provider. Rather than demanding our rights, we should turn to Him in humble dependence and expect that He will meet our needs. God created us and watches us so attentively that he knows the number of hairs on our heads. How could He not know if we need a good night's sleep, a warm bath, or a moment's quiet? As each of us learns to take up our cross and deny ourselves daily, let us also learn to wait only upon God—"for my expectation is from him."

My cup runneth over.

PSALM 23:5B, KJV

10

Planning a Wedding When Your Baby Won't Sleep through the Night

Being a Mother to Many Ages

I t was a rainy Friday in May 1998. I remember the rain clearly because our entire family was out in it, huddling together under a few overworked umbrellas. We had all traveled to Cedarville, Ohio, to attend Christy's college graduation that weekend, and we were getting the grand tour of the campus. "Up here is the new chapel and the library," Christy was saying, as we walked quickly across the damp sidewalks. "After this we can go to the cafeteria for some lunch." The younger boys, who had not been so enthusiastic about the campus tour, perked up at the sound of the word "lunch."

As we all trooped into the cafeteria and took off our soggy jackets, heads began to turn. I could see several of the students mentally counting children, and many smiled to see one-year-old Peter. Many of Christy's friends knew our family on sight from all the photos they had seen, and as Christy proudly introduced everyone, the little boys in particular became the center of attention. Although there were quite a few families of graduating seniors at the college that weekend, we certainly stood out. Among the families we encountered walking around the campus, eating in the cafeteria, or attending the graduation ceremony the following day, I saw few siblings under age twelve or so—and I did not see any other seniors who had siblings still in diapers.

Christy's graduation was one of those events that really remind me how unique our family is in today's society. Most of the parents at Cedarville College that weekend were in their final years of parenting. They were able to watch their children graduate with a bittersweet sense of accomplishment at a job well done. I, however, had only to glance at the long line of blond heads to my left during the graduation ceremony in order to see that I was only halfway finished!

Another difference that struck me was the level to which most of those parents had been able to be involved in their children's collegiate experiences. Although Mike and I probably brought one of the largest fan clubs to Christy's graduation ceremony, we had not been extremely involved in her college activities other than Mike's academic leading over the phone. When I attended the graduation, it was only the third time I had visited Christy's college campus—and it was the first time for most of the family. To some degree, I felt guilty knowing that many of Christy's classmates had received all sorts of parental care packages, letters, and visits during their college years.

I had similar feelings just a few months later, as Christy prepared for her August wedding to Rich Shipe. At the time, Peter was sixteen months old, but he was still not sleeping through the night on a consistent basis (my most difficult child in this area). Many were the mornings when I would be awakened by his cry, broadcast into my room by the merciless baby monitor, at 5:30—just five hours after I'd gone to bed. As I would stumble sleepily into his room, I remember thinking, "Here I am trying to help my oldest daughter plan her wedding, and my youngest son isn't even sleeping through the night yet! What's wrong with this picture?"

I struggled with trying to be involved in the wedding-planning process while continuing to care for the rest of the family, and functioning on little sleep. Fortunately, Christy is a very capable and independent sort of person, and she did very well handling most of the wedding plans herself. However, I would sometimes feel a bit "out of it" when my friends would say things like, "Wow, I bet you're really overwhelmed planning this wedding on top of everything else!" Although I did get to go shopping for wedding dresses and help with several of the details, I was not quite as involved as I had hoped to be. The same was true when Katie got married that October—perhaps even more so, because by then the school year had already started.

There is no doubt that being a mother to older and younger children simultaneously presents a unique challenge. At times I wonder if having younger children is keeping me from being a good mother to my older children. Unlike some mothers, I have not been able to attend every soccer game, ballet rehearsal, or piano lesson. Fun outings as a family and field trips to the many historical sights in this area have been difficult because of babies who needed naps and younger children who fussed and were not at all interested in what we were doing. I have not had lots of one-on-one time with each child individually, especially as they have grown older. And now that my children are having children of their own, I have not yet been able to spend as much time with my grandchildren as I would like.

In addition to my desire to spend sufficient time with each of my children, there are other challenges in raising teens and toddlers together. I have often struggled with putting together Bible lessons that will interest and instruct both sixteen-year-olds and two-year-olds at the same time. I have also wondered if my older girls feel burdened by too much responsibility in caring for their younger siblings and helping around the house. "Is a big family really best for my older kids?" I have fretted. "Would I be a better quality mother if I didn't have so much quantity?"

The More, the Merrier!

It has actually been my older children themselves who have allayed many of my worries in this area. I have often heard them say that, rather than feeling neglected, having a lot of younger siblings simply makes them feel that "there's more love to go around."

My own observation has borne out this statement. It has been a true joy to me to see the interaction of my children, especially the older siblings with the younger. For many years, Christy, Jayme, and Katie have been involved with the younger kids in many ways that I was unable to be—from taking trips to the amusement park to coaching soccer teams to reading adventure stories aloud. Christy has taught piano lessons to her younger brothers and sisters, Jayme has baked gingerbread houses with the younger children at Christmastime, and Katie has enthusiastically attended just about every sports game in which any of the children have ever played (even when her baby was two weeks old!). This is an obvious blessing to my younger children, but it has also blessed my older children in many ways.

Each of my three oldest daughters has often told me how much they enjoy their younger siblings. Especially during the sometimes-unstable teenage years, the unconditional love and acceptance of a child can be especially meaningful. Although Christy, Jayme, and Katie usually had good Christian friends during their teen years, even these relatively mature circles of friends certainly had their share of pettiness, fickleness, and instability. It was always refreshing for them to come home to the open arms and funny antics of their little siblings, who loved them no matter what.

Believe it or not, the little children have also played a positive, key role in the courtship of each of my three oldest daughters. Whenever Rich, Sean, or Todd would "come calling," they were immediately pounced upon by the little boys and asked to wrestle, race, or jump on the trampoline. This was a great icebreaker for these young men during the sometimes-awkward early stages of courtship, as well as a great chance for us to see how they held up under fire. The little children also made excellent "chaperones" for outings, giving these young couples a chance to do something together in a fun, nonthreatening family setting.

While Christy, Jayme, and Katie certainly did some complaining about all the work they had to do when they were growing up, they can now testify that the responsibility of a large family was overwhelmingly positive for them. (I would love to have had the knowledge they do when I first got married!) Besides knowing how to cook, clean, change diapers, teach children, do laundry, and wash dishes, they also know a great deal about bearing with all sorts of different people in patience and love. The same thing is quickly becoming true about Jessica and Angie as well.

Another thing that often develops in big families is that the older children become natural teachers of the younger ones. I have seen this attitude become evident in each of my oldest five daughters, as they have taken an active interest in the development of the younger children.

Many of my children have learned how to say new words, how to tie their shoes, how to throw a softball, or how to drive a car under the instruction of an older sibling. Several of my children have even accepted Christ after hearing the gospel from an older sister or brother.

This teaching spirit in my older children makes it easier for me to solve the dilemma of planning our "Special Time" for such a variety of ages. When I know that my older children are interested along with me in the development of their younger siblings, it is easier for me to plan activities, songs, and stories that are focused on the little ones. When we do sing a more childish song or tell an elementary Bible story, I try to involve my older children as teachers rather than simply as participants. At the same time, I always try to have some elements of our Bible time that are targeted toward my more mature children—and the little ones simply have to stay quiet for a short time, even if they do not fully understand.

As I have seen my three oldest daughters become adults, the evidence shows that they have certainly not been "scarred for life" from growing up in a large family—far from it. Each of them still spends a great deal of time at our house, playing with the younger kids, who are now aunts and uncles to their children. Perhaps the very fact that Christy and Katie started having children as soon as they were married is the most convincing proof that their childhood was a happy one.

The interaction between my children is a blessing to me just as much as it is to them. On holidays and weekends, at soccer games, or during evenings gathered at

226 A MOM JUST LIKE YOU

home, I love to just sit and take it all in. Mike is talking politics with one of my sons-in-law; another is tickling both Jon and Joe at once; Christy, Jayme, and Katie are laughing in the kitchen; Jessica and Angie are each holding a little niece; and everyone else is applauding Peter as he demonstrates his amazing jump off the coffee table. It is times like these when I truly feel that "my cup runneth over." There is something very satisfying and secure about being a part of a big, loving clan like this one—and I consider it to be a wonderful reward from God for letting Him do our family planning.

Psalm 133 speaks of the sheer pleasantness of family unity (both spiritual and natural) in poetic terms:

> Behold, how good and how pleasant it is
> For brothers to dwell together in unity!
> It is like the precious oil upon the head,
> Coming down upon the beard,
> Even Aaron's beard,
> Coming down upon the edge of his robes.
> It is like the dew of Hermon,
> Coming down upon the mountains of Zion;
> For there the Lord commanded the blessing—
> life forever.

Although my individual time with each child is somewhat limited, I truly believe that our corporate time together as a family unit has been an overwhelming blessing and source of love in the lives of each of my children. In addition to two loving parent/child relationships, each of my children has nine loving sibling relationships as well. And when we are dwelling together in unity, this is truly "good and pleasant" beyond measure.

WHAT ABOUT ONE-ON-ONE TIME?

The fact that the number of children in our family has decreased my individual time with each child does not mean that it has eliminated this time entirely—nor should it. I want to know each of my children on an individual basis, and any time I can spend with them one-on-one is very precious. There have been a few ways that Mike and I have worked to get to know each of our children individually, and to make them feel individually unique and special.

One thing Mike often does is to take one child on a trip with him. On several occasions he has taken just one or two children with him on a business trip to California or Florida, stopping at amusement parks along the way. Each of the older children has been on a trip to Europe with Dad (except Katie, who got married instead). This year it was Jessica's turn. This is a great way for Mike to get some individual time with his children, even in the midst of a busy travel schedule.

Back when Mike was not quite so busy, he kept a tradition for many years of taking one child to breakfast on Saturday mornings. This was always a special time for both the kids and him, and I'm always in favor of keeping a family tradition or two.

My individual time with the children usually comes in a more natural, unplanned way, as we are at home together throughout the day. I never have to work at spending time with my youngest children and babies, since they naturally have the most needs and demand the most of my time. For my school-age children, our home schooling provides me with a good chance for some one-on-one time on a daily basis. Because I teach each of my children one a time, I get at least an hour alone with each child every day. This gives me a chance not only to correct their schoolwork and give new assignments, but also just to chat with them a little, see how they are doing, and get a little glimpse into their minds and hearts. I also occasionally take one of my school-age children with me on my daily walk (usually when it's too dark to go alone and Mike is unavailable). They enjoy coming with me, and I enjoy the time to focus solely on them for an hour.

My daily walk has also been a great way for me to spend time with my oldest daughters. They seem to have inherited my love for the outdoors, as well as my desire for exercise, and I am sometimes joined by one, two, or all three of them. It has really been fun to see my relationships with Christy, Jayme, and Katie moving from a pure mother/daughter level to more of a peer level. Although they are certainly still my daughters, in some ways I feel like I have sisters for the first time. As we talk about our day, our struggles, our walks with the Lord, and our relationships with husbands and family members, I am greatly encouraged both by the fellowship and by the fact that my children have become such good friends. My individual time with them as children has now blossomed into adult friendship, and this, I believe, is the ultimate goal of parenting.

Working to Raise Adults

Older children can certainly bring a lot of joy, but they can also present great challenges. As difficult as it can be to parent small children, I believe most parents face the really tough issues when those children reach the brink of adulthood. For several years, I worried that I was allowing my older daughters either too much or too little freedom, and I just prayed that they would turn out okay. Their lives today are certainly an answer to that prayer.

Mike and I often hear from distraught parents who are struggling with the same fears and praying the same prayers for their older children. Indeed, young people today are facing a world that bombards them with choices that we could not even imagine when we were growing up. The increasing filth in music and movies, the mixed bag of opportunity and danger that is the Internet, and the general decay of popular culture can bring many parents close to panic. How can we protect our teens unless we are with them twenty-four hours a day?

While home schooled teens may not face the same level of temptation as their public schooled peers, there are still many cultural issues to be faced. Standards of dress, for instance, can be a problem area in many parent/teen relationships (home schooled or not). Then there are the questions of friendship and dating, which parents cannot afford to ignore or avoid.

On several occasions, Mike and I have heard from parents who were struggling with the issue of setting rules and standards:

"Our daughter wants to start wearing makeup, but we think she's too young."

"Well, he's been e-mailing this girl for a few months, and I don't know what they talk about. Should we be worried?"

"We just think her clothes look rebellious."

"He says that music is Christian, but I can't even understand the words."

These are all tough issues and questions, and neither Mike nor I have any "pat" answers to them. In many cases it will depend solely upon the family and the teen in question. If you're hoping to read a dissertation on what is and is not acceptable for Christian young people, you won't find it here! I believe there can be as many different standards and opinions on these issues as there are Christian families. However, I would like to give you a few underlying principles which Mike and I have used in raising our children, specifically in the area of standards, rules, and responsibility.

The most important principle I would share with you is this: our ultimate goal is not to raise children, but to raise adults. We want to eventually bring our children to the point where they set their own standards, make their own decisions, and take responsibility for their own lives. In other words, we want them to become adults. Our children are really children for only a while (shorter than many of us think) and during that time it is our responsibility to give them the tools they will need in adulthood.

There are two main ways parents can fail in this area: They can make the mistake of releasing their children into adulthood too soon, or they can release them too late. The former are parents who give up all rights to guide or discipline their children when the children are still very much in need of parental guidance. These parents will say, "We just don't want to alienate him," or "We don't know how to handle her otherwise." Unfortunately, these children are given rights without responsibility, and they enter adulthood expecting life to be handed to them on a silver platter.

I see the second type of mistake far more often in the home school movement. By their very nature, home schooling parents tend to be very involved in their children's lives. Unfortunately here, what often begins as a decision to do what is best for their children can also appeal to their desire to be in total control of them. Parents who yield to this desire tend to set arbitrary and inconsistent rules for their children and become upset and possessive whenever a child pursues desires that do not fit into the parents' plan. I have seen families where this happened, and the results were often tragic. Far too often, these young people were the very ones who fell into the hands of the world from which they had been so sheltered. Because they had never made their own decisions or learned the reasons behind their parents' decisions, they were ill equipped to deal with the temptations of the world around them.

Releasing our children into adulthood is not something that happens all at once. Rather, it is a gradual process (and it starts earlier than you might think). Before our children can be released, they must first be equipped (just as baby birds must first be fed and nurtured before they are pushed from the nest). So what can we be doing to equip our children for adulthood? Here are four suggestions that Mike and I have learned from our own experience.

First, maintain a balance between rights and responsibilities. All children need some rights and some responsibilities, but how many depends on their level of maturity. A child's rights and responsibilities should remain proportional to one another, and both should increase as a child matures. Your two-year-old probably has few responsibilities. He does not have to do much work around the house, he has no regular chores, and he has no schoolwork to study. In proportion with this low level of responsibility, he should also have a low level of rights. He should not determine his diet, his outfits, or his schedule. He should not be given everything he demands.

As much sense as this makes with a two-year-old, however, think how ridiculous it would be with a sixteen-year-old. At that age, our children should neither be waited on hand and foot nor be told exactly what to eat, what to wear, or how to plan their day. Instead, they will have guidelines or expectations in those areas, such as "food should be healthy," "clothing should be modest," or "you should make good use of your time." If your children have been well trained in the general principles, they need to be given the responsibility to carry out those principles for themselves. Otherwise, the principles will remain only theory, and your children will not learn how to put your standards into practice when you are not around.

Rights without responsibility will spoil our children. Responsibility without rights will never teach our children to actually be responsible, and it may embitter them toward us. Children get that final "push" into adulthood when they are finally given all rights and responsibility, but a good parent will have been gradually increasing the level of both from the time their children were young.

Second, let your children know at an early age what you expect of them, and be as consistent as possible. One family I know has several troubled children. They have tried one panacea after another in the hope of finding a solution for their family problems. As a result, they have changed churches and family standards many times over the past few years, and this has understandably been very difficult for the children. What was acceptable two years ago is now taboo, although next week it may be acceptable again.

While most of us will not go to this extreme, we will run into conflict if our children are sixteen when we first hit them with, "Oh, by the way, we don't believe in dating." Now of course, some families may sincerely adopt new convictions in these areas when their children are older, and those families will have to work to make the transition as smooth as possible. However, it is ideal for us to consider these issues when our children are young and to tell them early what we expect of them.

Christy was eleven years old when Mike first took her out to breakfast and explained that courtship, not dating, would be the practice in our family. (This principle is explained later in this chapter.) As a result, she grew up knowing that she would not be like some of her friends, who were picking out boyfriends at age fourteen.

This is not to say that once you lay down an early rule, you can never "tweak" it as time goes by. Our courtship rules have changed a little through trial and error, and Mike's early declarations that none of our daughters would ever wear makeup have fallen by the wayside. In some ways, our younger daughters face a slightly different set of rules than our older daughters did (and this did elicit a few eruptions from them). However, we have tried to remain as consistent as possible throughout the years, especially in the most important areas.

Third, have reasons for your rules, and tell your children what those reasons are. Obviously, I am not saying that you always have to explain to your four-year-old why he can't buy a new action figure. For young children, "because I said so" can often be a sufficient reason, and they need to learn and honor that.

While older children should also honor and obey their parents, remember that your ultimate goal is to equip them for adulthood. To do this, you need to tell them not only what the correct decisions are, but how you came to those decisions. Mike and I always endeavor to tell our children (especially our older ones) the biblical and practical reasons behind the standards we set. As a result, our oldest children have now adopted most of these standards and principles as their own (not because we said so, but because they found our standards to have intrinsic merit). This, of course, implies that your standards will have valid reasons behind them. As you make decisions about family standards, be sure to have a solid basis (preferably a scriptural one) on which to stand. Those standards and rules which are based only on your personal taste should certainly be obeyed while your children are under your authority, but they will probably be the standards which your children are least likely to adopt as their own.

I have known families who got into serious conflicts with their children over issues that seemed to me somewhat trivial. In one family, the parents preferred tailored clothing, while the daughter wanted to wear long, flowing dresses. The daughter's taste in clothing was not immodest, it was just different from her parents' taste. Now, while I am by no means advocating rebellion on the part of the daughter, I do believe we parents would do well to pick our battles in these areas. It is highly important for us to maintain a good relationship with our children and to nurture their unique personalities.

It is sometimes difficult to separate personal preference from a biblical standard, as I found out in my own life. Nevertheless, when you and your older child differ on an issue, ask yourself whether you are differing on a standard of biblical truth or propriety, or whether it is merely a matter of personal taste or preference. Your children should obey the rules that you set up, but if your rules are designed to make your child a miniature version of yourself, you run the risk of creating bitterness and resentment.

Paul's words to the Ephesians on this issue were very wise: "And, fathers, do not provoke your children to anger; but bring them up in the discipline and instruction of the Lord" (Ephesians 6:4). Arbitrary rules can provoke our children to anger, but rules based on the clear instruction of the Lord will produce God-fearing, parent-honoring children.

Fourth, establish a trust relationship with your children based on their love relationship with God. This is the most important principle. Our ultimate goal with our children should be to make rules obsolete, because they are completely guided by their own walk with the Lord. When our children walk closely with God, we can trust them to obey His standards for behavior. When they know that we trust them, they have an even greater motivation to maintain and honor that trust.

When children are young, most of their obedience is motivated by the fear of punishment. There is nothing wrong with this at a young age, but we certainly want our children to reach the point where they are motivated for other reasons. We have to realize that there will come a day when we can no longer discipline our children (for one thing, they often grow to be bigger than we are!). If by the late teenage years we have failed to lead them into a solid relationship with Christ and into a good, loving, trusting relationship with us, they will be very hard to reach.

There were many occasions during our daughters' teenage years when we saw the importance of their love relationships with both God and us. When Christy was eighteen, she voluntarily came to Mike and me and confessed that, unbeknownst to us, she had begun a "boyfriend/girlfriend" relationship with Rich Shipe. They had been writing and calling each other for the past several months, and they had both expressed feelings beyond friendship to each other. While Mike and I were obviously somewhat upset by this news, we were also grateful that Christy had finally been convicted to come to us on her own. We certainly had no idea what was going on, and she probably could have kept the relationship undiscovered for a quite a while longer. Nevertheless, both her relationship with God and the knowledge of her parents' trust caused her to come to us in openness and honesty.

For several years, I struggled with my daughters in the area of music. Although I recognized that our musical tastes were very different, I also felt that some of the music they listened to was probably not pleasing to the Lord. I maintained my standards in this area as long as I could, but my daughters finally reached an age when I simply had to let this issue go and leave it in God's hands. As usual, He dealt with things much more capably than I could. Jayme was eighteen when she went on her first mission trip to Romania. The day after her return, I noticed her hauling a large plastic garbage bag out to the garage. The contents of the bag clattered noisily as she walked past. "What are you doing, Jayme?" I asked. She smiled at me a little sheepishly. "Well, I just feel that God wants me to get rid of all my secular tapes and CDs. So I'm throwing them all away." She glanced at the bag with some reluctance. "It's not like I think all of them are intrinsically wrong, but I feel like it's a little test for me from God and I just need to do it."

It is when my children make decisions motivated by their love for God that I feel I have truly succeeded. I can only be in control for a short while, but if I succeed in introducing my children to the living God, I know they will be in good hands.

The Importance of Communication

As your children mature spiritually, your own relationship with them should also naturally move in an upward spiral. As you come to trust them more, they in turn should be able to trust you more in sharing their thoughts and hearts. Sadly, I have seen some parents who, despite the fact that their children were relatively mature, seemed to always expect them to mess up rather than trusting them to honor the Lord. As a result, the children resisted sharing anything with their parents for fear that they would find fault in whatever they said. The parents, in turn, saw that their children were not talking to them and trusted them even less, thus creating a downward spiral.

Parents who act this way do so because they want to keep their children from falling into sin or trouble.

However, I believe that trust is a much more powerful tool in accomplishing this aim (assuming the child has been well trained and has a relationship with the Lord). For one thing, young people who know their parents trust them will be very reluctant to destroy that trust, and if they disobey their parents, they will be quickly convicted by the knowledge that they have abused their parents' trust. On the other hand, children who know that their parents expect them to disobey often feel that they might as well fulfill those negative expectations. They feel they can't do anything right no matter what they do, so why bother.

Trust, however, does not mean that you should fail to make your children aware of how easy it is to fall into sin. It will be equally harmful to your children if you act as if they are incapable of sinning. Rather, be realistic about temptation, expect honor and obedience, and keep lines of communication open. Being transparent about your own weakness and need for God will help them to rely on God themselves, and it will also make it easier for them to come to you when they are facing temptation.

I can think of no other area where a trust relationship is so important as in the area of dating and courtship. As I mentioned earlier, our family does not follow the widespread American practice of "dating" as it has come to be understood. Rather, our children maintain friendships (and no more) until they are ready for marriage and have found one specific person whom they believe would be a good life partner. With the full approval, guidance, and involvement of both sets of parents, this young couple then moves into what we call "courtship" (which is basically a commitment to get to know one another with the stated purpose of possible marriage).

There are too many good books on courtship to make it necessary for me to explore this subject in depth. Mike has actually written a more detailed explanation of our family's courtship principles in his book, *The Home Schooling Father*. However, I simply would like to point out that your child's spiritual maturity and trust relationship with you will be more important to the whole courtship process than any specific set of rules.

In fact, the actual practice of courtship has been a little different for each of my oldest three daughters. Although the general principles remained the same for all three, their unique personalities and stages of life made the "rules and regulations" somewhat different for each of them.

When Christy came to us at age eighteen and told us of her mutual emotional attachment with Rich Shipe, Mike was not exactly pleased about this at first. He saw some areas of immaturity in Rich's life (not surprising for an eighteen-year-old). Feeling that Christy and Rich were not at the stage of life when they were ready to get married soon, Mike asked them to refrain from all one-on-one contact, which at the time consisted mostly of letters and phone calls. Shortly after this, both Christy and Rich left for separate colleges; she went to Ohio, and he went to Pennsylvania. They had basically no contact with each other for a year-and-a-half.

I got a phone call from Christy near the end of her freshman year of college. "Mom," she said, "I don't know how to say this, but I still really have feelings for Rich. I've been struggling about this all year. I know you thought I might think differently once I 'got out' a little, but being around the guys here at college has only convinced me more that Rich is the one for me."

Since Christy and Rich had not communicated for a year, I was impressed that she still felt so strongly about him. Although Christy had not asked me to, I talked to Mike that night about the possibility of their being able to communicate again. Mike was also impressed. I think he thought, like me, that Christy's little "crush" would pass as soon as she and Rich were separated. Mike was even more impressed, however, by the fact that Christy and Rich had honored his request and refrained from communication. He decided to let them write each other again.

Over the next three years, Christy and Rich's relationship grew. They started "officially" courting in the summer of 1996, although the courtship mindset had really been in place the entire time. They were engaged on Christmas Day 1997, and married in August 1998 (much to the delight of both Mike and me).

Katie's courtship with Sean Dunn was quite different. Mike liked Sean right off the bat, and he was delighted when Sean started coming over to our house and hanging out with our family. It was not too long before Sean and Katie started to become good friends (playing with the kids together, coaching a softball team together, and sharing a similar sense of humor). Given the fact that Katie did not have too many solid Christian friends at the time, we were especially happy to see her growing friendship with Sean. However, we wondered whether we should be worried about such a friendship, because at the time Katie was only fifteen. We made sure that all their activity was in a family setting, and at one point we limited the amount of time they could spend together.

Nevertheless, by Katie's sixteenth birthday it was clear that nineteen-year-old Sean had long-term intentions toward her. He spoke with Mike that year about the possibility of beginning an "official" courtship with Katie. After Mike and I did a lot of thinking, praying, and searching Scripture, we really felt that Sean and Katie were ready to take this step. Katie had always been mature for her age, and it was clear that her friendship with Sean had brought about a lot of spiritual growth in her life, as well as a closer relationship with Mike and me. We truly felt God had brought these two together, and we gave our permission for them to begin courting.

Unlike Christy and Rich, whose relationship was a long-distance one, Katie and Sean spent most of their time together at our house. This family setting allowed Mike and me to provide some guidance for their activity, but the younger kids made things very fun and non-threatening. Katie also took several trips to Texas to spend time with Sean's family. Sean and Katie were finally engaged in April 1988 and married that October.

Jayme, who tends to be less independent and strong-willed than Christy or Katie, surprised us by being the last of the three to develop a relationship. At the beginning of 1996, when she was eighteen, she came to Mike and me and told us that she had decided to dedicate the next two years to specifically focus on serving God. This meant she would not begin or even consider any romantic relationship during that time. She felt that she had things to accomplish before she would be ready for marriage, and a specific commitment made it easier to keep her mind focused on those things. Mike and I gave her our blessing and waited to see what would happen.

Jayme's next two years were primarily spent doing mission work in Romania. Her first trip was in May 1996, and then she spent all of 1997 living in the city of Oradea. Strangely enough, there were a few young men who approached Mike about Jayme during the year she was overseas. However, she stuck to her commitment and would not even seriously consider anything until her two years were up, in January 1998. Upon her return, she continued to exhibit little interest in any relationships, although she did have a few opportunities. Mike and I were not worried. She still seemed to be very open to the idea of marriage, but I did start to wonder what kind of a young man Jayme would find acceptable.

This continued throughout 1998 and into 1999. In the meantime, Jayme stayed very busy with her various activities and missions work. At the same time, she had several good friends, both male and female, which was something we had always encouraged for each of our daughters.

Early in 1999, however, Jayme surprised us greatly by telling us that one of her friends, Todd Metzgar, was becoming a bit more than a friend. He came and talked to Mike shortly thereafter, and they started courting in April. Their courtship has been a little different, also, because they are both somewhat older (she is 22; he is 27) and in the stage of life when they are ready to get married. Mike and I have continued to oversee things; and again, most of their time spent together occurs at our home. However, we have also felt a little less need to supervise all activities. Todd and Jayme were engaged in December 1999 and are planning a wedding in June 2000.

Obviously, our daughters' courtships have not been one-size-fits-all, and I believe this is how it should be. However, in each courtship we endeavored both to adhere to our general principles and to keep open lines of communication. From time to time Mike and I would go for a walk or to dinner with our daughters and future sons-in-law to discuss the relationships and find out how they were doing. At other times they would voluntarily come to us to share things. At all times, however, we sought to maintain an atmosphere of trust based on their individual relationships with God. We were able to do this because we started early equipping our children with the tools for adulthood (and most importantly, introducing them to Jesus Christ).

Because I saw how important it was for my older children to be spiritually mature, I am now even more motivated to continue nurturing my younger children spiritually. But I am also encouraged that, despite my mistakes, fears, and worries, God is faithful to answer a mother's prayers.

"Thou hast given him his heart's desire, and hast not withheld the request of his lips" (Psalm 21:2).

Her children rise up and bless her; her husband also, and he praises her, saying: "Many daughters have done nobly, but you excel them all."

PROVERBS 31:28-29

11

EXCHANGING AMBITION FOR SERVICE

The Eternal Value of Motherhood

S o, what do you do?"

Although this is an extremely common way to "break the ice" in modern conversation, I still never know quite how to respond. Most people today think of themselves in terms of what they do, but I think of myself more in terms of who I am: I'm a mother. However, "I'm a mother" is not always a satisfying response to this question. Far too often, I still see expectation in the questioners' eyes, as if they are waiting for the other shoe to drop. The implication is, "Okay, you're a mother, and…?"

It's true that motherhood is no longer as totally despised as it was in the heyday of feminism. In fact, in some ways it is coming back into fashion. We hear more and more about the importance of "parental involvement" in the lives of children. Many of the women who are praised as role models today have motherhood listed as one of the accomplishments on their resumes. However, the motherhood that is in vogue today is a far cry from what was once the ideal. Today, instead of just being a mother, you have to be a mother and.

I am sure you may have read the articles or seen the news stories about these celebrated women: devoted mom and Hollywood actress, mother of two and president of an international relief organization, loving mom and U.S. congresswoman. Today's women, we are told, can and should do it all. They can be excellent wives, exemplary mothers, and outstanding leaders in the field of business, culture, or education.

Unfortunately, the modern church has all too often fallen into this way of thinking. Women who are simply mothers, and who have a large number of children—the thinking goes—are limiting their potential to serve God. They could be leading Bible studies, doing evangelistic work, traveling to distant corners of the world, or devoting themselves to church activities. Instead, they are stuck at home washing dishes and changing diapers. What a waste!

I have talked quite a bit in this book about the fact that the rewards of home schooling and motherhood are worth the sacrifice. The time you get with your children, their little tokens of affection, and the lasting impact you can leave on their lives are all ample rewards for the nausea of pregnancy, the late nights with little babies, and the loss of free time in caring for little ones. When your children grow into mature, God-fearing adults, you reap the full fruits of your labor—and they are sweet indeed.

However, even if we believe that we ourselves will be emotionally rewarded for our sacrifice, we may still struggle with this nagging thought: Couldn't I have done something better with my time? Wouldn't I have had more impact on the world if I had pursued a public career or ministry? Is "just being a mom" a selfish choice after all?

When I was young, I had the vague but strong desire to "make a difference" in the world. Even before I became a Christian, I had thoughts of becoming a missionary or a dedicated teacher, doing something grand and glorious that would impact the lives of others. Later in life, when Mike and I made the decision to trust God with our family size, I thought my dreams of making a difference had pretty much ended. Although I was still convinced that God wanted me to give Him control of my womb, I thought a large family would certainly limit my ability to serve Him.

Home schooling and mothering my large family have limited my opportunities to do things outside the home. I have not had the time to do much community outreach, organize many church activities, or even be a very vocal encouragement to my fellow home schooling moms. Even this book would not have been written or published if my daughter and I had not worked on it together.

God has surprised me, however, by allowing me to impact the world through my children in ways I never would have thought possible. Although I never really expected my life to make much of a difference, He has shown me the extreme importance and eternal value of servant-motherhood.

"JUST A MOTHER"

The Bible and history are full of examples of women who impacted the world solely through motherhood. These women not only raised children who changed the course of history, but they also made a tremendous contribution to their children's success.

Without his mother's bravery, Moses would have died as an infant, and without her faithfulness, he would never have been trained in the knowledge of God. Hannah had a tremendous impact upon Israel through her son Samuel, by earnestly praying for his birth and bringing him to serve in the temple at a young age. Ruth went from being a widowed foreigner to mothering the grandfather of the great King David—who was in turn an ancestor of Christ. Timothy came to know Christ under the diligent instruction of his mother and grandmother. These women are known for little more than their commitment to children and family, but who can calculate the eternal impact they had through simple maternal faithfulness?

We see similar examples of invaluable motherhood when we look at more recent history. Susanna Wesley, already mentioned, gave birth to nineteen children—ten of whom survived infancy. Among those were John (number 15) and Charles (number 18), well-known leaders of the Great Awakening. Not only did Susanna Wesley bear a great number of children, but she was also highly involved in both their academic and spiritual training. Imagine if "family planning" had existed in Susanna Wesley's day, and she had been given the chance to limit her family to two or three children. Would she have used that opportunity, and if so, how could we measure what the world would have missed?

Several years ago on Mother's Day, I received a small booklet entitled *Called to Be Mothers*, written by one of my favorite authors, Elisabeth Elliot. Mrs. Elliot, the widow of missionary Jim Elliot, is known and respected by Christians all over the world for her outstanding public ministry. She began her missionary career alongside her husband Jim, who was tragically killed by the Auca Indians of Ecuador when he was still quite young. Incredibly, Mrs. Elliot returned to those very Indians who made her a widow, and she lived with them for a number of years, teaching the love of Christ. Since her return to the United States, she has been a prolific author and public speaker and has encouraged and challenged believers of all ages.

Because I knew Mrs. Elliot's background, I was astounded to read the following statement at the end of her *Mothers* pamphlet:

[God] calls some to be single, some married people to be childless, but He calls most women to be mothers. There are, the Bible tells us, "differences of gifts," and they're all given to us according to God's grace. None of the gifts of my own life—not my "career" or my work or any other gift—is higher or more precious to me than that of being someone's mother.

I thought this was an absolutely incredible thing for Mrs. Elliot to say! Just think of the implications of her statement. She considers the highest and most precious gift in her life to be the gift of motherhood, above and beyond being a missionary, a well-known speaker and author, and an example of godliness to women around the world. And she only had one child! This was a tremendous encouragement to me as I was sometimes tempted to doubt the importance of what I was doing.

As I think of the eternal value of motherhood, I am reminded of the most renowned and revered mother in all of history. Mary was just a young Jewish girl, betrothed to be married, when she first learned from the angel Gabriel that she was to be the mother of God's Son. A virgin, Mary was obviously very surprised by this news and possibly a little distressed about what it implied for her future. She had no way of knowing that this pregnancy would not ruin her socially, destroy her hopes of marriage, and make her an outcast. I doubt she even fully grasped all that her Son would be and do for the entire world.

However, once she heard the word of the Lord through Gabriel, she responded in faith with these humble words: "Behold the maidservant of the Lord! Let it be to me according to your word" (Luke 1:38, NKJV). Mary could not have foreseen all that God would do with the fruit of her womb. I am sure she was somewhat confused; she was probably a little frightened. But she knew that God had given her a job to do, and she trusted Him both to protect her and to carry His work out to completion. She did not ask, "How am I going to serve the Lord simply by delivering a child?" Rather, Mary was faithful to do her part of the work, and she left the rest up to God. Recognizing her own "lowly state," (Luke 1:48) Mary considered herself blessed just to bask in the reflected glory of her Son. She did not seek to be recognized in her own right. As Elisabeth Elliot writes in *Called to Be Mothers*, "she was willing to be known as, simply, Someone's mother."

Mary's humble acceptance of God's plan for her is an example to each of us. God knows better than we do how we can best serve Him. When He gives us marching orders, it is not for us to second-guess Him or offer better suggestions for how we might best advance His kingdom. We would do much better to respond, with Mary, "Behold the maidservant of the Lord! Let it be to me according to your word." Just as Mary brought God's Son into the world through her humble submission and acceptance of motherhood, so we can bring God's Son before the world by doing the same.

AN UNLIKELY IMPACT

When Christy was a student at Cedarville College, she came home each year for the week of spring break—and her sophomore year was no exception. As usual, she was accompanied by her roommate Laurie, a native of Washington State who could not always make it home for school breaks and holidays.

That year, however, we ended up with a few more guests than we had originally expected. Just a day or two after Christy got home, she received a phone call from her friends Jeff and Tim, freshmen from Cedarville. They had planned to do some sightseeing on the East Coast during spring break, and Washington, D.C., was their first stop. Unfortunately, they had unexpectedly run short on finances and were unable to pay for a hotel room. Would we mind, they asked, if they slept at our house while they were in the D.C. area? We told them we were happy to oblige, as long as they didn't mind sleeping on the family room floor!

Jeff and Tim spent two days with our family and seemed to thoroughly enjoy the kids, even though Jon and Joe got a little rough at times. However, I was surprised when, a week after the end of spring break, a letter from Jeff arrived in the mail. As I opened and read his letter, I couldn't help smiling. The letter has been one of the permanent additions to my "encouragement file" ever since. Jeff wrote:

Dear Mr. and Mrs. Farris,
Thank you so much for allowing Tim and I to

stay with you two days last week. You have no idea how much that helped us out, not only in just having fun, but also with our financial situation, since we obviously did not have to pay for a motel room those nights. I really did enjoy staying at your house and had a lot of fun. From the active alarm clock in the morning (Jon jumping on me), and surviving all of the "attacks," I had a blast.

It's really good to know that there are solid families out there, and I hope that one day I will be able to have a hair of what you and your family have. To be honest, Tim and I talked about how cool we thought that your family was all the way to Charlottesville. You did a great job with your kids. (Although you're probably thinking that "it's not over yet"). Anyway, thank you for showing me (I'm pretty sure that I can include Tim in this) what a good Christian home can be like. Thanks again for everything.

I certainly had not spent hours talking to Jeff and Tim about the value of a strong, godly family. However, our family itself spoke more clearly than any lecture from me ever could have. We never know what kind of an impact we are having on those around us, just by faithfully doing what God has called us to do. Simply being there, raising a godly family, can be a tremendous ministry.

I have seen this to be true on other occasions as well. I often hear from home schooling moms across the country who know of me through Mike's work. Sometimes I get letters from these women through HSLDA; other times I meet them on the rare occasions when I attend a home school conference. I am amazed by how many women have told me, "It encourages me so much just to know you're there, doing what you're doing." This is both humbling and heartening for me. Only God could use my ordinary life to reach people I have never even met and to encourage them as they follow Him.

Like those women of Bible times, I also am often able to see myself reaping a spiritual harvest through my husband and children. Mike, Christy, Jayme, and Katie have been able to go places, do things, and share Christ in ways that I certainly could not have done as one person. As Jesus told his disciples in John 12:24, "Truly, truly, I say to you, unless a grain of wheat falls into the earth and dies, it remains by itself alone; but if it dies, it bears much fruit." Our death to our own "self-fulfillment" can actually bear more fruit than we would have borne alone. Again, we see that, measured by human wisdom, God's ways are upside-down. What human would ever say that the path to spiritual productivity is death? But Jesus Himself proved to be the ultimate example of this truth.

When people ask us how we can be productive for God if we are saddled with all these children, we need to remember that God is the one who brings about spiritual productivity. I believe we modern believers would do well to relearn the truth of 1 Corinthians 3:7, "So then neither the one who plants nor the one who waters is anything, but God who causes the growth." Far too often we act as if we are in control of the growth of God's Kingdom. But He simply calls us to faithfully sow, water, and harvest, and to leave the results up to Him. We do the work we are assigned to do; God gives the increase.

As in farming, sometimes the increase may be different than we expect it to be. When George Washington Carver first began to teach his agriculture students about the importance of rotating crops, many people thought he was crazy. Sweet potatoes and peanuts? What could you do with those useless crops? Cotton was king! However, Carver's critics finally learned that such crops enrich the soil with vital nutrients, which eventually lead to a much richer, more productive cotton crop.

In the same way, we may not always feel like the daily work we are doing is yielding much for the Kingdom. Our kids are taught, fed, and bathed; our dishes are washed; our laundry is done—but so what? Little do we know that these simple acts of service are enriching the "soil" of our children's lives to produce a tremendous harvest. God has a way of using our service in ways we wouldn't expect—and could never have imagined.

WHAT GOD VALUES MOST

I learned an important lesson shortly after the birth of Emily, my seventh child. Emily proved to be one of my fussiest babies, and I spent the first several weeks of her life doing little but walking her around, trying to get her to stop crying. Only when she was sleeping did I get a break from that nervous energy of hers, which demanded so much of my attention.

As the fussy days turned into fussy weeks, my frustration mounted. Once in a while, I would have to lay Emily in her cradle and let her scream, because I was getting too annoyed to keep holding and calming her. Not only was Emily's crying taxing my patience, but I also felt that I was accomplishing absolutely nothing. "What use am I to anybody, sitting here keeping this kid from crying?" I thought to myself. "What a useless life!"

During that time, I was reading through a book that contained a series of devotionals for new mothers. One day, I came across a devotional that I have remembered ever since. It was based on Jesus' words in Matthew 10:42, "And whoever in the name of a disciple gives to one of these little ones even a cup of cold water to drink, truly I say to you he shall not lose his reward."

Little things are of tremendous value to God. The world would think little of someone who simply gives a cup of cold water to a child, or who spends days and weeks caring for a fussy baby. But God looks on such service as so valuable that those who perform it are assured of a reward from Him. Giving a cup of cold water to a little one is surely one of the most simple, basic, and unglamorous acts of service that anyone could perform. Surely God also highly values our simple, basic, and unglamorous care for our children on a daily basis. I was so encouraged to learn this lesson, and I remembered it on many occasions afterward.

Obviously, God's value system is different than ours. He values the "little things" just as much, if not more, as the "big things." He is looking for simple faithfulness. I remember attending a conference at which Elisabeth Elliot was the keynote speaker, and I will never forget her remarks on what God values most. "It is a far higher act to do what God wants us to do than to be creative," she said. "To will the will of the Father is far greater than the greatest piece of art."

I have often thought that, once we get to heaven, we may be very surprised to see who receives the highest honor. I have sometimes pictured what such a surprise might be like—the saints all gathered around the throne, receiving golden crowns for their earthly faithfulness. As the Lord draws out one of the biggest and most jewel-laden of the crowns, the throng wonders which saint has earned it. Surely it must be someone very special, very notable and admirable. But as the Lord calls the name of the crown's owner, everyone thinks, "Who?" The throng parts, as a little gray-haired woman steps forward. She is the faithful nursery worker, or the prayer warrior who spent hours in her living room lifting up the needs of the world, or the simple woman who always opened her home to whomever needed a warm meal. No one had ever regarded her as particularly important or influential, but in God's value system she is worthy of high honor.

Jesus Himself imagined such a scene, when he was instructing the multitudes in Matthew 25:34-40:

"Then the King will say to those on His right,
'Come, you who are blessed of My Father, inherit
the kingdom prepared for you from the foundation of the world. For I was hungry, and you gave
Me something to eat; I was thirsty, and you gave
Me drink; I was a stranger, and you invited Me
in; naked, and you clothed Me; I was sick, and
you visited Me; I was in prison, and you came to
Me.' Then the righteous will answer Him, saying,
'Lord, when did we see You hungry, and feed
You, or thirsty, and give You drink? And when
did we see You a stranger, and invite You in, or
naked, and clothe You? And when did we see You
sick, or in prison, and come to You?' And the
King will answer and say to them, 'Truly I say to
you, to the extent that you did it to one of these
brothers of Mine, even the least of them, you did
it to Me.'"

Jesus counts service done for any of His brothers,
"even the least of them," to be service done for Him.
Surely our own tiny, dependent, needy babies and little
ones are among "the least of them"! Don't ever believe
that your small acts of simple motherhood are of little
value in God's sight—no matter how the world's value
system may belittle them.

Indeed, in every passage that describes women who
are of high value to God, we see women who are busy at
home, who excel in simple acts of service and kindness,
who possess good character, and who minister to others

from their homes. Titus 2:3-5 is one of the passages where God indicates what He considers to be important for women:

> Older women likewise are to be reverent in their behavior, not malicious gossips, nor enslaved to much wine, teaching what is good, that they may encourage the young women to love their husbands, to love their children, to be sensible, pure, workers at home, kind, being subject to their own husbands, that the word of God may not be dishonored.

You may notice that while this list does not prohibit community service or ministry outside the home, these things are not deemed to be of the highest importance, especially for women whose children are still young. When we make our children and home our first priority, we should not feel that we are second-class servants of God—not in the slightest! No matter what those in the world or even in the modern church may say, God highly values a woman who cares for her husband, children, and home. To be exact, He estimates her value as "far above jewels" (Proverbs 31:10b).

I think it would help us understand why God values faithful mothers so highly, if we would simply imagine a society where every mother placed her husband, children, and home as her first priority. Can you imagine the strong marriages and well-adjusted, happy children which would result? If every mother would simply give of herself to raise children who will in turn give, and not take, from society, there would be much less need for outside ministry in the first place. It is precisely because families are broken, marriages are torn, and children are hurting that our world has such a need for ministry and service.

As long as you are imagining a better society, picture this: what if every Christian family in American history had just been faithful to teach their beliefs to their children? America started out as an overwhelmingly Christian nation; today only wishful thinkers would ever say that this is so. If today's "remnant" of Christianity would make the sacrifice it takes to instruct their little ones in God's ways, I believe we could see a vastly different America after only a few generations.

When we raise godly children in the midst of a hurting world, we are striking at the very root of the problem. We are not just treating the symptoms; we are treating the disease. "Just being a mother" is far from inconsequential!

AMBITION VS. SERVICE

In emphasizing the value of simple motherhood, I am not saying that God does not call some women to do other things in addition to their mothering. In fact, I don't believe that motherhood and ministry, or even motherhood and business, have to be mutually exclusive. We see many examples of women in the Bible who, while first caring for the needs of their families, have also turned their homes into centers of business or ministry.

While the Proverbs 31 woman "works with her hands in delight," "gives food to her household," "grasp[s] the spindle," and "opens her mouth in wisdom," she also "extends her hand to the poor," "makes linen garments and sells them," and "considers a field and buys it; from her earnings she plants a vineyard."

Similarly, in 1 Timothy 5:9-10, we see that God values a woman "having a reputation for good works; and if she has brought up children, if she has shown hospitality to strangers, if she has washed the saints' feet, if she has assisted those in distress, and if she has devoted herself to every good work."

I believe the common thread among these examples of industrious women is that they make their families their first priority, and their primary ministry center the home. It is clear that a woman who stays home is certainly not disqualified from having a vital ministry. Rather, by providing a godly, well-run home as an oasis from the world, she can minister both to her family and to others.

Remember, however, that the reason for taking on secondary projects or ministries is not to "validate ourselves," or to prove that our lives have some usefulness. We have already seen how highly God values our service as mothers. We should have no need for self-validation, because we are already doing something of eternal worth.

Rather, our ministry should be motivated by the same thing that motivates our motherhood: simple service for the Lord. We are here to advance His agenda, not our own. Oftentimes when we think of "advancing our own agenda," we picture someone who is ambitious for money, fame, and power. We can clearly see that this kind of ambition is wrong. However, it is far too easy for us to fall into another kind of ambition—the ambition to be recognized for our achievements for God and to serve Him for the sake of feeling good about ourselves. If we do things for God simply to be able to pat ourselves on the back, we are headed for a trap. The devil can be very subtle in twisting humble service into prideful service. When you feel yourself thinking, "I could serve God better without these kids," ask yourself, "What is my motivation for service?" Is it truly to advance God's aims alone, willingly accepting the role to which He has assigned you in accomplishing those aims? Or is it to advance your own "spiritual ambition" in order to gain human recognition? As unpleasant as this second motivation may sound, it is amazing how often it will find its way into our subconscious minds.

My dictionary defines ambition as "a strong desire for fame, success; honor, wealth, or other position; seeking after a high position or great power." I was struck by how completely opposite this attitude is to that of Christ, who said, "For even the Son of Man did not come to be served, but to serve, and to give His life a ransom for many" (Mark 10:45). Service is the essence of the Christian life; ambition is the antithesis.

Recently, I read a news article about an earthquake that hit Athens, Greece, in September 1999. As rescue workers searched for survivors, they found a ten-year-old boy who had been trapped beneath a collapsed apartment building. The boy's injured father was also there, holding up a beam to keep it from falling and crushing his son. Incredibly, this man had been holding up the beam for over 24 hours. The pair was pulled free, but the father later died from his injuries. Although the news item I read was brief and factual, I found the tears coming to my eyes as I thought of this father's self-sacrificial love for his son. In a way, I felt his sacrifice was symbolic of true parental love. When we have children, we are placed in the position of standing between our children and the harsh world that threatens to crush them. We can bear the weight of this responsibility with bravery and love, or we can let go in order to "fulfill ourselves" or "realize our dreams." One Greek father literally gave his life to protect his son—but he was able to save his son's life in the process. This is surely the most lasting impact any parent could make on his child: to give him additional years of life and breath. Without his father, this little boy's life would have been cut short.

We, too, seek to eternally impact our children for good, to protect them from an evil world and train them so they can eventually be a light to that world. For us, the cost of making this impact will probably not be so high—we will probably not have to literally die. Nevertheless, we will have to die to ourselves, our ambition, and the praise of men. In doing so, we will probably have days that are utterly devoid of glamour, where we do nothing but wipe runny noses, change smelly diapers, and wash dirty dishes. But no matter how lowly the world may view those tasks, God highly values those who perform such basic acts of service. In trading ambition for service, we will win praise from the living God. And we shall surely not lose our reward.

"His lord said unto him, Well done, good and faithful servant; thou hast been faithful over a few things, I will make thee ruler over many things: enter thou into the joy of thy lord" (Matthew 25:23, KJV).

The lines have fallen to me in pleasant places; indeed, my heritage is beautiful to me.

PSALM 16:6

12

STRONG TREES FROM SMALL SEEDS

The Vision of a Spiritual Heritage

There are times when the end of a task has a bitter-sweet taste. When someone leaves a job, even if it is to move on to a better job or into retirement, he can still feel somewhat wistful as he cleans out his office and says goodbye to his former coworkers. Although in one sense he is grateful to have finished his work there, he also faces the uncertainty and even the emptiness that often come with change. His daily routine—and by extension, his life—will be a little different now. He only hopes that he did his best, and that he trained his successor to continue the work he began.

I experienced those feelings to a small degree this year, as I helped at the births of my first two granddaughters. As I witnessed the nervous excitement of my daughters and sons-in-law, as I helped coach my daughters through contractions, and as I watched the nurses begin warming blankets just before each baby arrived, I was transported back to all the mixed emotion of new motherhood. Although I couldn't help but be reminded of the pain and exhaustion that come with labor, I was also reminded of the overwhelming joy when I first held my baby in my arms—a joy that far outweighed all the pain.

The day Katie was in labor with her first daughter, Jenna, I took a little break from labor coaching to go on a walk with Mike around the hospital grounds. Having just come from the familiar sights and sounds of the delivery room, I was somewhat contemplative. "Don't you think it's a little sad," I mused, "to think that we will probably never be in that place again—having a new little baby? It just feels like life is changing—our kids will be having the babies now—and it seems a little sad to me."

"Well," Mike replied, "I know what you mean—life is changing. But I don't think we've really come to an end of being fruitful. I think we've just moved on from one phase of fruitfulness to the next. I mean, we're participating in our second birth this year—that never happened when you and I were having kids. Instead of slowing down, we're just going to be having more babies than ever coming into the world!"

I nodded, still not totally reassured. "Think of it this way, Vickie," Mike continued. "God told mankind to 'be fruitful and multiply.' For years we have been working on obeying the first part of that command, and we have been very fruitful. But now we've moved on to the 'multiplying' part—and that's exactly what we're doing. Our family is growing exponentially!"

As I thought over these words, I found myself greatly encouraged by them. Mike and I hadn't stopped being fruitful; we were simply being fruitful in other ways—and, I might add, we were more fruitful than ever. Because we had raised up successors, our work was continuing on an even larger, more widespread scale.

I am sure I will again experience bittersweet emotions when I reach the end of my home schooling years, although with my youngest only two years old, that day is still a long way off. Nevertheless, that day will eventually come, and I know I will have feelings of wistfulness and regret as I finish a task that has consumed so much of my day-to-day life. As hard and challenging as some days have been, and as much as I have sometimes longed for a break from home schooling, I know I will greet the end with some sadness when it actually does arrive.

At that time, however, I believe I will again be comforted to see my children walking in my footsteps, and continuing even further down the path I walked, as they home school their own children. Instead of being just one family training our children in righteousness, Mike and I will have duplicated ourselves many times over. Just as one who finishes a job trains a successor to carry on his work, so we should aim to produce children who will "carry on the torch" of faithful obedience to the Lord. In fact, our goal should be to produce children who carry that torch even farther and better than we were able to carry it.

A few months ago, Mike preached a sermon about spiritual productivity. In it, he used this analogy: "Imagine that we are apple trees, and we want to produce as abundant a harvest as possible. The best way to do that is not simply to grow more apples, but to produce more apple trees. We want our children not just to be apples, but to be apple trees—to carry on the work of productivity." Just as God has designed all living things to reproduce themselves physically, so He wants His people to reproduce themselves spiritually. The Bible is full of examples of this kind of spiritual reproduction. Abraham passed the covenant on to Isaac, who passed it on to Jacob, who passed it on to his sons, who fathered the twelve tribes of Israel. In this way, God's covenant with one man became God's covenant with an entire nation.

Elijah spent several years training Elisha to be God's prophet to Israel. After Elijah was taken up to heaven, his well-trained successor carried on his work. In fact, Elisha was given a double portion of Elijah's spirit, and God enabled him to perform twice the miracles and wonders that Elijah had.

The Christian church itself is the result of this same kind of spiritual reproduction. Jesus could have made his earthly ministry a "solo act," traveling the country alone as He preached, healed, and taught. Instead, He chose to take twelve men under His wing and train them to carry on His message after He returned to the Father. Jesus' twelve disciples became the founders of the early church, and they in turn trained others to "go and make disciples of all nations." Jesus' planting of the Gospel into the hearts of twelve men continues to bear fruit all over the world today.

I would like every home schooling mother to catch this same vision of raising "a godly seed"—a seed which will continue to reproduce itself and bear fruit long after we are gone. There are few things more tragic than Christian workers whose service for God dies with them. However, by our very nature, we mothers have a tremendous opportunity to produce successors who will not only carry on our work, but who will actually continue it on a much larger, more widespread scale than we were able to do.

It isn't easy for us home school moms to see the "big picture" or maintain a long-term vision when we're so caught up in the busyness of our daily lives. As we correct schoolwork, wipe up messes, and discipline fighting children, it's difficult to feel like we're part of a big, exciting plan to impact future generations. Maybe we can envision our own children turning out well, and thus repaying us for our hard work, but that's about as far as our imaginations take us.

As rewarding as it is to see our children walking with God, I believe He wants to extend this heritage of godliness to our grandchildren, great-grandchildren, and generations yet to come. As happy as we are to see our own household living in righteousness, God can turn our righteous household into a righteous community, and eventually into a righteous nation. In this final chapter, I would like us to look at this "vision of a godly seed," and to see how God can use our short-term faithfulness to produce a long-term harvest.

A GODLY HERITAGE TAKES HARD WORK

Just a few weeks ago, I gave a short devotional at a baby shower for Christy and her daughter Emma. As I gathered Bible verses about the blessing of children in preparation for the devotional, I turned to one of my old favorites, Psalm 127:3. "Behold, children are a gift of the LORD," my Bible reads. "The fruit of the womb is a reward." When I looked at this verse in the King James Version of the Bible, however, the wording was slightly different: "Lo, children are an *heritage* of the LORD: and the fruit of the womb is his reward" (emphasis added).

The word heritage struck me, because at that very same time I was involved in a women's Bible study on the book of Joshua. A few days before, our Bible study had met to discuss the first chapter of Joshua, and much of our discussion had centered on the idea of the Promised Land as Israel's heritage. Specifically, we had talked about the fact that although God had given Canaan to the Hebrews as an inheritance, they still had to do a lot of hard work in claiming that inheritance. In order to possess that which was rightfully theirs, the people had to actively cross the Jordan, enter the land, and conquer the Canaanites.

Our Bible study had also mentioned that the same thing is true of our spiritual inheritance in Christ. Although our acceptance of Jesus' payment for our sin guarantees us "an inheritance which is imperishable and undefiled and will not fade away, reserved in heaven for you," (1 Peter 1:4), we are still instructed to "work out [our] salvation with fear and trembling" (Philippians 2:12). Our old nature is still with us, and we must actively walk in the Spirit in order to be truly in possession of our spiritual inheritance. A heritage is not something we gain quickly or easily!

Now, as I looked at Psalm 127:3 in preparation for Emma's baby shower, I began to reflect on children as a heritage rather than simply as a gift. Although I enjoy thinking of my children as a gift from God, the word heritage is an even richer and more fitting description of what our children are to us. Just like the Israelites' heritage of the Promised Land, the heritage of children is one that brings with it a lot of hard work. But the more work we invest in our children, the better the inheritance will actually be.

Imagine a man who inherits an estate, but who never bothers with the upkeep it requires, and it soon falls into disrepair. He will still own it, but eventually he will have decreased the value of his own inheritance. When his own life ends, he will not have much of a heritage to leave his family after him. However, if he diligently manages the estate, he can actually increase its value as time goes by, leaving his children an even better inheritance than he himself received. The value of the heritage increases with the work invested.

How true this is with our children! When you make the decision to stay home with your children, and to take the responsibility for their education, you have made a tremendous commitment to give of yourself in order to invest in their lives. However, the more work you invest, the greater your inheritance will be, and the richer your heritage in generations yet to come.

We also see this concept of hard work when we look at the second half of Psalm 127:3, which tells us "the fruit of the womb is his reward." I had always thought of a "reward" simply as something nice that God gives us, like a blessing. However, when I looked up the Hebrew word, I discovered that the word used in Psalm 127:3 is often translated "wages." The idea is that our children are payment given to us in return for our own hard work.

It is true that just pregnancy itself requires quite a bit of work, not to mention labor and delivery. Holding our newborn baby is the first reward we receive for our perseverance and sacrifice. However, I believe this process of labor and reward continues throughout our children's lives. We need to remember that the full reward of children doesn't come for free, nor does it come right at the beginning. It is given to us in return for our diligence throughout the years.

If you are at the point where you are not feeling particularly rewarded by your children, I encourage you to persevere. Know that your hard work is earning a reward, which will surely come if you don't give up. Of course, it is also encouraging to know that we receive little rewards for our work along the way. The more time we invest in our children, the more rewards we will start to see. For the mother who is faithful during the "planting" years of hard work, there will come a day when her life will be simply overflowing with the fruits of her labor.

Children are indeed a heritage from the Lord, and the fruit of the womb is his reward. Let us work hard to claim our inheritance and care for it as a valuable possession.

The Rich Rewards of a Lasting Legacy

Another aspect that distinguishes a gift from a heritage, in addition to the amount of work required in possessing it, is the length of time it will last.

In general, a gift is usually something temporary in nature. It could be a piece of clothing or perfume or chocolates or money—but a gift is usually not around forever. Neither is it something that takes a long time to earn or purchase. Our family has set some speed records buying gifts on the way to birthday parties and wrapping them in the car! In the grand spectrum of things, a gift is for the short term.

However, a heritage is something which both takes a long time in coming, and lasts a long time after we receive it. The son who will inherit his father's estate must first spend many years learning how to handle the finances and oversee all the details of managing the estate. He then must still wait until his father's death to fully inherit all rights to the estate. But after he does gain his inheritance, he will have it for the rest of his life (assuming he manages it well), and will in turn pass it on to his son. With continuing good management, the estate could stay in the family for countless generations to come.

Likewise, the blessing of children does not come overnight, but neither does it quickly disappear. Children take a long time to develop and mature, and we must spend a lot of time and energy in training them. However, once they are well-trained, they will bring us a lifetime of joy. Even after the end of our lives, our children will live on and probably have children of their own. Like a heritage, our children are the "gift that keeps giving," even into generations yet to come.

It is not only our children's ability to extend our family line that makes them a long-lasting gift to us. Children are the one thing we receive from God, besides salvation, which will last into eternity. Each of our children has an eternal soul which can never be extinguished. And when each of those eternal souls is won over for the Lord, we can indeed leave a long-term legacy.

As a young person, did you ever dream about the legacy you would leave, or the impression your life would make on the world? I believe many of us have had the desire, especially when we were young and idealistic, to leave a lasting impression on history. Maybe we wanted to write that great American novel, or become a famous celebrity or sports star, or rise to political power. I believe when young people dream of "leaving a legacy," they often think in terms of fame, wealth, and power.

However, even those who do reach such goals rarely leave an impression that long outlives them. How many of us can name James K. Polk's vice president, or rattle off the top Academy Award winners in 1963? History ultimately determines which legacies truly deserve to be called legacies, and which ones are merely passing moments in the spotlight.

I believe the surest way to leave a lasting legacy is much more quiet and unassuming than winning the vice presidency or an Academy Award. When we raise children who love the Lord and want to serve Him, we can truly touch the future for good. Our children may be the only lasting legacy that we leave, and they have the potential to carry our names, our family traditions, and our commitment to Christ into untold generations.

Children are the bridges that connect the past with the future, and descendants keep cultures alive. However, descendants can carry on their unique heritage only when they are truly immersed in that heritage, trained in their mother tongue, and aware of their cultural identity. The same is true of families as well as nations. Our children can carry on our spiritual heritage (not to mention our family name and identity) into the next generation only if they are fully immersed in the ways of God.

The Jewish people are perhaps the best example of this truth. The Old Testament placed a heavy emphasis on parents training their children in the law, talking of it throughout the day, binding it on the forehead, and writing it on the doorpost. In addition, God gave the

Israelites an abundance of signs, symbols, and festivals to remind them—and especially their children—of their covenant with God and their unique history.

When God ordained the Passover celebration, He gave the people this admonition:

> "And you shall observe this event as an ordinance for you and your children forever. And it will come about when you enter the land which the LORD will give you, as He has promised, that you shall observe this rite. And it will come about when your children will say to you, 'What does this rite mean to you?' that you shall say, 'It is a Passover sacrifice to the LORD who passed over the houses of the sons of Israel in Egypt when He smote the Egyptians, but spared our homes.'" (Exodus 12:24-27)

The Passover was designed expressly as a tool for parents to familiarize their children with the story of the Israelites' flight from Egypt. Through this celebration, an entire people still remembers an event that took place centuries ago.

No ancient nationality or faith has been preserved as the Jews and Judaism have. We no longer have Hittites, Ammonites, or Jebusites, but we still have Jews. Even though the Jewish people have been widely persecuted and scattered throughout the world, their unique cultural identity has remained intact. Of what other people group could we say the same thing? I believe the Jews have retained their heritage partly due to divine protection, but also due to the fact that parental training of children is imbedded into their culture. As a result, this tiny group of people has overcome unparalleled persecution to become one of the longest-lasting, most influential people groups in the world.

We have this same potential to spread the message of Christ throughout the world simply by being faithful within our families. Because we serve the same God that the ancient Hebrews did, we also have His divine methods for leaving a vast spiritual legacy. I doubt that the ancient Hebrew mother, who taught her children as she baked bread, swept the house, and beat out the rugs, had any notion that her people would still be thriving two thousand years later. Neither is it easy for us, as we teach our kids phonics and feed them peanut butter sandwiches, to see just what God can do through our faithfulness. I firmly believe that, through us, God can touch future generations in mighty ways.

"Like arrows in the hand of a warrior, so are the children of one's youth," Psalm 127:4 tells us. "How blessed is the man whose quiver is full of them; they shall not be ashamed, when they speak with their enemies in the gate" (verse 5).

Indeed, the analogy of arrows is very apt to describe the widespread and distant influence our children can have. After we have fully trained them, "aiming" them at the mark of Christ, we can them set them loose to fly toward the target. As we send forth our children, they can reach people and places for Christ that we ourselves could never have reached. Our sphere of influence and our ability to "do battle" for the kingdom of God is dramatically increased when our quiver is full of these little "arrows." Not only can we send them forth into a multitude of new places, but we can also send them forth into future generations to do the work of the Lord.

MAKING DISCIPLES OF NATIONS

Mike and I were recently visiting with some friends who serve as missionaries to Mexico. Mike and Pam Richardson are the home schooling parents of seven children, and they have been in Mexico six years now. God has used them to establish a very effective ministry to win entire Mexican families for Christ through evangelism, discipleship, and training. The Richardsons have a special focus on aiding Mexican families who desire to train their children through home schooling.

So far, Mike and Pam have seen God do mighty things as they work both to bring the Mexican people to Christ and train Christian families to disciple their children. I believe the fruits of their ministry will only increase as the children from those believing families grow up and begin godly families of their own.

Far too many mission boards look at children as hindrances to ministry, who should be limited in number and shipped off to boarding schools as soon as possible. However, the Richardsons have established a very effective ministry with their children as active participants. A hurting, broken Mexican family could take one look at the unity, discipline, and love in the Richardson home and notice the difference of Christ. Mike and Pam's large family is central to their ministry, both in helping them identify with the predominantly Catholic Mexican people, and in setting an example of what a Christ-centered home can be.

What's more, Mike and Pam's seven children are actively involved in evangelizing, preaching, running the printing press, and otherwise serving in their mission work. I have no doubt that many—or all—of them will end up on the mission field themselves in their adulthood. Who can predict the mighty things that God can do in years to come through this one family?

The problem of broken, hurting families is a universal one. Now more than ever, people need to see homes where Christ is central, parents love each other, and children are trained in the nurture and admonition of the Lord. People who are seeking solutions for their family problems cannot help but be drawn to those who seem to have found the answer. Our families, in addition to being training grounds for our children, can also be a very effective testimony of God's power even while our children are still young.

There is great potential for godly families to reach the world with the Gospel simply by living faithful lives before the world. Mike likes to point out that when Jesus told his disciples to "go therefore and make disciples of all the nations" in the Great Commission, He didn't say to make disciples in nations, but to make disciples of nations. What is God's way for creating a discipled nation? It's easy to see, through His dealings with the

Hebrew people, that a discipled nation was to be made up of discipled tribes, which were in turn to be made up of individual families. When we faithfully work to produce discipled families, God can increase both our number and our influence, causing us to grow into discipled nations.

Home school families are sometimes criticized by the modern church as being too "withdrawn" from the world to shine the light of Christ. However, I believe our very separateness is what helps light remain light in contrast to the darkness. Families who shine forth the light of Christ are becoming much rarer—and thus much more noticeable—in today's dark world.

I recently attended a conference for leaders of home school organizations across the country. One of the keynote speakers at the conference was Paul Weyrich, founder of the Free Congress Foundation and one of the most influential conservative voices in Washington, D.C. Addressing an audience of long-time home school leaders, Weyrich spoke of the decay that is widely evident in American society today. Although he remains politically active himself, Weyrich told the audience that he no longer believed politics, or government, were going to provide the solution for the nation's ills. Rather, he said that he felt the change must come from within the culture itself, and that Christians must take the initiative to transform popular culture from the inside. Rather than castigating home schoolers for "withdrawing" from society and contributing to the decay, Paul Weyrich praised the home school movement for providing a valid alternative to the failing public school system. He compared home schoolers to the underground church in the former Soviet Union.

"I have recently traveled to the former Soviet Union and seen the Christian church coming alive there," Weyrich said. "The church is now filled with young people where there once were only old women. So I decided to ask some of these Christian young people how they knew they were Christians after so many years of Communism. In every single case the answer was the same: 'My grandmother.' Even as the nation was listening to the Communists shout, 'There is no God!', these old women would whisper into the ears of their grandchildren: 'Remember we are believers. There is a God, and we believe in Him.'"

Weyrich continued with an analogy: "Even though the Russian church remained hidden beneath the decaying structure of Communism for so many years, as soon as that rotten outer shell fell away, the church was there to shine the light and fill the cultural void."

I was struck by the imagery of this analogy. Like those old Russian grandmothers, we home schooling moms are building a counter-culture beneath the rotting structure of today's American society. Our faithfulness is creating a sound structure that, by the grace of God, will last even after the rotting outer shell of our culture has crumbled away. We are not "abandoning ship"; rather, we are building a lifeboat.

When God ordained a nation to be "His people," through which He would bring salvation to the entire world, He deliberately made them very distinct from the world around them. They had a set of laws, customs, ordinances, and festivals which were downright bizarre to the nations around them. For many years they didn't even have a king! And yet it was through these "strange" Jews that Jesus came, bringing salvation for the entire world.

This does not mean that we have no contact with the world around us. "You are the salt of the earth," Jesus said. However, He immediately followed this statement with a warning: "But if the salt has become tasteless, how will it be made salty again? It is good for nothing anymore, except to be thrown out and trampled under foot by men" (Matthew 5:13). When we spend intensive time with our children during their formative years, training them in the word and ways of God, they will more easily retain their "saltiness" when they are sent out to flavor the world. Moreover, as we reap the natural benefits of home schooling—like family closeness and unity—the world cannot help but notice something different about us.

The life of a home school mom is about much more than textbooks and dirty dishes. As we ordinary home school moms give of ourselves to create Christ-centered homes, we show the self-sacrificial love of Jesus to a hurting world. As our children grow, they can go forth into the world as "arrows in the hands of a mighty warrior." And as our grandchildren and great-grandchildren are trained to serve God, our spiritual heritage can become deeper, richer, and more widespread throughout our community, our nation, and even our world.

Indeed, the vision is amazingly large. But I believe it can be realized as we rely on the extraordinary power of God to work through our ordinary lives. Remember that all the daily, mundane elements of your life—the schedule, the curriculum, the late nights and early mornings—are simply playing a tiny part in the mighty plan God has for your family and His kingdom.

Let's remember this truth and keep our perspective during the hard days. No test score, kitchen floor, or casserole will prove our ultimate worth or success, nor does the power of God lie in these things—although He may use them. Just as Christ both used and transcended earthly elements like loaves, fishes, water, and wine, so will He both use and transcend the simply little acts of faithful service that mark our daily lives. God can do extraordinary things through moms just like you. I am confident that as you yield to Him, even in your frustration, fatigue, and weakness, He will use you to impact the world in mighty ways. God can grow strong trees of righteousness—a mighty spiritual heritage—from our small seeds of service. Until then, let's simply be faithful to plant, water, and weed, expectantly waiting for God to give the increase.

"And let us not lose heart in doing good, for in due time we shall reap if we do not grow weary" (Galatians 6:9).